# The Growth of Self-Insight

LEO M. FRANKLIN – 1870-1948

# THE GROWTH OF SELF-INSIGHT

*The Franklin Memorial Lectures*
*Volume X*

*Edited by* JOHN M. DORSEY
*Holder of the Leo M. Franklin Memorial Chair in Human Relations at Wayne State University for the year 1959-1960*



DETROIT—WAYNE STATE UNIVERSITY PRESS—1962

*Library of Congress*
*Catalog Card Number: 61–18939*


*Wayne State University Press*
*Detroit 2, Michigan*

*Published simultaneously in Canada*
*by Ambassador Books, Limited, Toronto, Ontario, Canada*

The lectures in this volume were broadcast locally by WDET (Wayne State University), nationally through the facilities of the National Association of Educational Broadcasters, and internationally by the Voice of America.

*The Leo M. Franklin Lectures and the Occupants of the Leo M. Franklin Memorial Chair in Human Relations at Wayne State University*



† Out of print. * To be published in 1963.

Titles of volumes differ in some instances from titles of lectures as originally announced.

# *Preface*

Detroit's Temple Beth El and Wayne State University honored the memory of a great rabbi and cultured gentleman in 1950 by establishing a chair in his name: the Leo M. Franklin Memorial Chair in Human Relations. Each year the Franklin Memorial Professor, a member of the faculty recommended by a faculty committee and appointed by the president of Wayne State University, organizes and presents a series of lectures featuring the principle of humaneness. It is my privilege to be named Franklin Memorial Profesor of 1959-60, by President Clarence B. Hilberry. Each of my co-authors, Professors Harold A. Basilius, Bernard Mayo, Milton Rosenbaum, and Wilbert Snow, readily and ably directed his devotion to his work-up of the idea: the growth of self-insight. The fact cannot be emphasized too much that every human being can *increase* his self-insight. He can realize Lessing's definition of life as an education for humanity. It will not be necessary for him to live his life out lacking in a true self-estimate, to deprive himself of the life-giving appreciation of what it means to be a human individual, provided that his mind will discipline itself with the truth of self-consciousness. Jefferson saw, " Health is no more than learning."

My lecture series has benefited greatly from the helpfulness of Winfred A. Harbison, vice president for Academic Administration, Wayne State University; Richard C. Hertz, Rabbi of Temple Beth El, Detroit; Gordon H.

Scott, vice president for Medical College development and dean of the College of Medicine, Wayne State University; Charles A. Lewis, assistant director, Publication Services, Wayne State University; Walter H. Seegers, professor and chairman, Department of Physiology and Pharmacology, College of Medicine, Wayne State University; Mrs. Barbara Woodward, assistant editor, Wayne State University Press; and Mrs. William A. Bostick and each Faculty Women's Club Committee member.

My wife's clear awareness of the preciousness of complete individuality is most congenial to my efforts to grow my self-insight.

JOHN M. DORSEY

# *Contents*

# Introduction

# *Introduction*

He scales the heights of human bound
Who trains his sights to view the ground
of selfhood.

THESE LEO M. FRANKLIN Memorial Lectures in Human Relations of 1960 complete a decade of this effort devoted to education to humaneness. Previous holders of the lectureship and the general titles under which their lectures were presented are listed in this volume. Every year's lecturer has exerted faithful effort to exalt the humanitarian principle. Highminded and lowly wise Dr. Franklin sensed practicality in the cultivation of his own humanity, for observing his fellow man as himself. Said he, " In a word, man is the supreme teacher of man. The rabbi, therefore, must above all be a psychologist, able to read himself into the place of other men."

As noted, each preceding lecture series focused interest upon the nature and benefits of the humane way of life. This present series is an effort to report upon the law accounting for humaneness itself, for:

(1) the amount of humaneness already existing, and
(2) the method for increasing that amount.

Investigation of these two meaningful (mindful) areas accurately describes my life work.

William Osler, beloved physician, recorded, " We forget that the value of a nation to the world is neither the bushel nor the barrel, but *mind*." The world is now tending to divide itself sharply into two major schools of psychology: communistic and democratic. The communistic school teaches that the human individual is an important part of the whole sovereign state in which he exists,—an insightless world-orientation. The democratic school teaches that the sovereign individual *is the whole* who lives his family, community, state, and world, within himself,—an insightful self-orientation. The reality test of the worth of each of these teachings is, Which way of living grows and distinguishes humaneness? Archibald MacLeish writes,

> Our reliance in this country is on the inquiring, individual human mind. Our strength is founded there: our resilience, our ability to face an everchanging future and to master it. . . . And we are free because it is the man who counts in this country: always and at every moment and in any situation, the man. Not the Truth but the man: not the truth as the state sees the truth or as the church sees the truth or as the majority sees the truth or as the mob sees the truth, but the truth as the man sees it, as the man finds it, for himself as man.[1]

In *A Report to the American Council on Education,* Daniel A. Prescott wrote for the committee, "If the schools of the various nations fail in their education for world citizenship, events will ultimately teach the ethical realities which exist—but it will be at a tremendous cost in human suffering and cultural loss."[2] The prerequisite for a pupil's studying and practicing himself in world citizenship is his learning in such a way as to see his world as his. This view is entirely original and new for each pupil as he creates it.

Why is the discipline of education not clearly recognized as the mind's concentration upon the healthfulness of learning, and the discipline of medicine not clearly recognized as the mind's concentration upon the learning of healthfulness? "By wonder are we saved," noticed Plato.

This nation's founders set up the wise citizenship goals of " life, liberty, and the pursuit of happiness." However, the realization of each of these goals is a product of each citizen's degree of appreciation of the helpfulness of each one of them. In the interest of his world's peace, it is most essential that every growing citizen give himself the opportunity to discover all that he is able to achieve by means of his insightful living, all that he is able to decide by means of his free will, and all of the enjoyable health he can create by means of observing the inviolability of his individuality. Above all it is essential that the growing infant and child citizen escape as far as possible having to associate blindly any kind of punishment (deliberate unkindness) with his loved ones. Thus conceived, continuous United States citizenship study is continuous education to mature mental health.

Radical reverence for human individuality necessitates tolerance of mystical meaning. Einstein observed, " The most beautiful emotion we can experience is the mystical. It is the sower of all true art and science. He to whom this emotion is a stranger, who can no longer wonder and stand rapt in awe, is as good as dead."

In his book *The Training of the Human Plant,* published in 1906, Luther Burbank deplored early educational experience of any formal kind, declaring, " The curse of modern childlife in America is over-education," and, " It is imperative that we consider individuality in children and their training precisely as we do in cultivating plants."

Said he, " Education gives no one any new force "; self-knowledge is not an acquisition of an extraneous power. Of the learning process he observed, " When this growth from within has been awakened and cultivated, thoughts live and are transmitted into endless forms of beauty and utility."

J. M. D.

# I

# Thomas Jefferson's Faith in Human Integrity

*by*
BERNARD MAYO

## *Thomas Jefferson's Faith in Human Integrity*

To SPEAK BRIEFLY on Thomas Jefferson is always difficult. One is embarrassed by the riches of the subject—by the universality of the man—by the magnitude of his activities and achievements. I have often thought how difficult it must have been for him to select, in his old age, only three of his manifold contributions to mankind to be inscribed on his tombstone—those three contributions for which he wished most to be remembered by posterity: "Author of the American Declaration of Independence, of the Statute of Virginia for Religious Freedom, and Father of the University of Virginia."

Jefferson has been called "the central figure in American history," the Apostle of Americanism, the Architect of Democracy. But he was also a world figure. An English historian recently has called him "the epitome and compendium of his age." He was indeed a foremost representative of the Age of Reason, of that eighteenth-century Enlightenment which was graced by other men of versatile genius including such titans as Goethe and Benjamin Franklin. His voluminous writings reflect the Enlightenment in his passion for universal knowledge, for scientific experimentation, for cultivation of the arts, for all the multitudinous aspects of human relations. They have been called the richest treasure-house of information ever written by a single man.

What Jefferson wrote and what Jefferson did have

pertinence to our time because he grappled with so many perennial issues involving basic human values. The continuing significance of the man has inspired an unceasing flow of biographies and special studies. Scholars have written monographs on him as statesman and political leader. But in addition they have explored and appraised his contributions as philosopher, scientist, architect, classical and religious scholar, bibliophile, agriculturalist, botanist, inventor, philologist, patron and practitioner of the arts, economist, educator—the list goes on and on, and is seemingly endless.

It would be a very bold man indeed who would attempt to take all Jefferson for his province within the time limit so drastically imposed by a lecture. But it may be possible within that time limit to speak to some purpose, on some few aspects of the man, if we can discover some common denominator of his thought and action. I believe there is such a key to an understanding of Jefferson, a central theme that gives his rich diversity a harmonious unity. And this becomes apparent if we concern ourselves not with what he did but with *why* he did what he did during his many-sided career.

The key to an understanding of Thomas Jefferson—the mainspring of his thought and action—is his faith in human integrity. This basic motivation, I believe, explains *why* he pursued all knowledge that bears on human behavior with such insatiable curiosity, such inexhaustible energy. This impelling cause explains *why* he made such broad-ranging creative use of that knowledge, applying it with unremitting zeal to advancing everything that gave promise, as he said, of "enlightening the mind of man, and improving him as a rational, moral, and social being."

His faith in human integrity is suggested by Woodrow Wilson's remark that " the immortality of Thomas Jefferson does not lie in any one of his achievements, but in his attitude towards mankind." Wilson's remark, however, needs more precise definition. Mankind to Jefferson was never some statistical abstraction but always the sum of living, three-dimensional, flesh-and-blood individuals. And the key to an understanding of the man was far more than his " attitude towards mankind."

It was, rather, a profound faith in the worth, and dignity, and intelligence of human beings that lies at the foundation of all democratic thought and action.

It was an unshaken faith that man was endowed with certain inalienable rights; that he was able to govern himself in human brotherhood under principles of reason and justice; and that he possessed innate potentialities for his individual good, and his social well-being, which were capable of indefinite improvement.

It was a courageous faith that required struggle against everything which obstructed the individual's fulfillment of his potentialities, emphasizing that the measure of an individual is the good he contributes to society. For Nature, according to Jefferson, " has implanted in our breasts a love of others, a sense of duty to them, a moral instinct; in short. . . . Nature has constituted *utility* to man the standard and test of virtue."

And finally, it was a robust faith deriving strength from the progress man very definitely was making in a New World environment, where he had been granted the great boon of starting afresh, given a new chance to prove his capabilities when freed from the dead hand of the past. America, this virgin land of freedom and hope and opportunity, was to be a model for the world. Here in the new republic—which Jefferson when president described as "a rising nation . . . advancing rapidly to destinies beyond the reach of mortal eye,"—men were pioneering a bright new future for all mankind.

While his faith in human integrity was glowingly optimistic, it was tempered by his critical realism. He was too much the realistic man-of-affairs, too much the critical student of the past and of his own times, not to acknowledge that man had his frailties as well as his nobler qualities. He well knew that man often did not act like the rational creature the Age of Reason assumed him to be, having been throughout history peculiarly susceptible to the forces of indifference, fear, folly, bigotry, and ignorance.

Nevertheless, he was convinced that man himself—by self-insight, self-education, self-discipline—could overcome these evil tendencies or at least divert or minimize them. He emphasized man's nobler qualities and constantly appealed to them to promote their development. He resolutely refused to believe that man, with all his faults and weaknesses, was incapable of rational, moral, and social advancement through the exercise of his will, his energy, his resourcefulness.

Great victories over the "tyrannies and oppressions of body and mind" are undoubtedly possible, he once said, "although I do not, with some enthusiasts, believe that the human condition will ever advance to such a state of perfection as that there shall no longer be pain or vice in the world." And again, he declared: "I am among those who think well of the human character generally." I believe that man's mind "is perfectible to a degree of which we cannot as yet form any conception. It is impossible . . . not to see what an immensity in every branch of [knowledge] yet remains to be discovered " and utilized. And " as long as we may think as we will, and speak as we think, the condition of man will proceed in improvement."

Freedom then, he fervently insisted, was essential if these glowing promises were to be fulfilled. Man must be freed from the bondage of ignorance and superstition, from tyrannies and oppressions whatever their guise or shape. Only the free man, with unobstructed access to knowledge, could develop his potentialities, liberate himself through education and understanding, and enrich his life and the lives of his fellow men. Only in freedom could man progress in his pursuit of happiness and virtue.

Thus Jefferson throughout his life, whether he was concerning himself with politics, education, religion, or science, had always before him one great objective: the freedom and happiness of man. And always, no matter what aspect of his career we may examine, we shall find that he was animated and sustained by his abiding faith in human integrity.

The roots of that faith go back to his student days in colonial Virginia—and, indeed, can be traced back to the foundations of our Western civilization. He had the great good fortune, so he tells us, to come under the influence of two inspiring teachers, George Wythe and William Small, who introduced him to the ideas of the Age of Reason, that was also an age of faith in man's possibilities. Of those youthful days he once said, in words that apply to his whole career: " I was bold in the pursuit of knowledge, never fearing to follow truth and reason to whatever results they led, and bearding every authority which stood in the way." In this spirit he embarked upon his lifelong and incredibly industrious process of self-insight, self-education and self-discipline, applying himself most faithfully to a program of studies encyclopedic in their breadth.

Then and later he displayed an amazing efficiency in so organizing his activities as to get the utmost out of every long and fruitful day. Then and later he was fond of saying that " Nature intended me for the tranquil pursuits of [knowledge], by rendering them my supreme delight." In his letters he would sometimes exclaim that music " is the favorite passion of my soul." And again, that his favorite passion was science, or agriculture, or mathematics, or architecture, according to the particular subject he was then pursuing with characteristic fervor.

When the Marquis de Chastellux visited him in the spring of 1782 he found a man who had so developed his potentialities as to be the very model of that eighteenth-century ideal, the well-rounded " compleat gentleman." Chastellux was impressed by the classic symmetry and elegant taste of Monticello, the mountain-top mansion Jefferson had designed and built. But he was even more impressed by Mr. Jefferson himself, " the first American who has consulted the fine arts to know how he should shelter himself from the weather."

This accomplished and scholarly Frenchman described his host as a tall man, not yet forty, with gentle manners, warm heart, and animated mind, who was at once an architect, philosopher, astronomer, musician, scientist, and statesman. Jefferson was a little reserved at first, but very soon " we were as intimate as if we had passed our whole lives together." On one memorable evening they drank punch and read the poems of Ossian, Chastellux reported, and by the mutual aid of punch and poetry " the night far advanced imperceptibly upon us. Sometimes natural philosophy, at others politics or the arts, were the topics of our conversation, for no object has escaped Mr. Jefferson; and it seemed as if from his youth he had placed his mind, as he has done his house, on an elevated situation, from which he might contemplate the universe."

Supreme as his delight was in contemplative scholarly pursuits, " the enormities of the times in which I have lived have forced me," said Jefferson, " to commit myself on the boisterous ocean of political passions." It was to be a long and stormy political voyage. On it he carried as chart and compass the philosophy he had developed during his early years. It stressed the freedom and good of the individual; and yet it also, and always, stressed the freedom and good of society—of individuals collectively. For the test of individual virtue, Jefferson was fond of repeating, is what the individual contributes to the good of society. As the scholar-in-action, as America's philosopher-statesman, he himself superbly met this test during his forty self-sacrificing years in active public service.

He began his political career in the epoch of the American Revolution, and he began it characteristically by affirming his faith in human integrity. He was a Virginia lawyer-planter in his mid-twenties when he was first sent to the colonial legislature, and there he attempted to make it legally possible for owners to emancipate their slaves. He did not succeed. Nothing liberal or humanitarian could then expect success, he tells us, under the imperial system of George the Third and his Tory ministers, whose continued violations of British America's natural and constitutional rights eventually brought on the war for independence.

His philosophy of freedom found eloquent and effective expression in this age of Revolution. In 1774, as a young legislator of thirty-one, he was determined to cut through all the legalistic quibbling which had beclouded the controversy with Britain for ten years past, and set forth fundamental rights in a bold and forthright statement. And this he most successfully did in his pamphlet, *A Summary View of the Rights of British America.* He appealed to King George in these ringing words: " Open your breast, Sire, to liberal and expanded thought. Let not the name of George the Third be a blot on the pages of history." And, anticipating the Declaration of Independence by two years, he asserted: " Kings are the servants, not the proprietors, of the people. . . . The God who gave us life gave us liberty at the same time; the hand of force may destroy but cannot disjoin them.",

Life and liberty, inseparably joined together—always a basic theme to Jefferson.

His revolutionary manifesto of 1774 flamed defiance. It caused Britain to list him as an arch-rebel. Yet it was written by a man noted in the ordinary affairs of life for his gentleness, his courtesy, his adherence to his maxim: " Take things always by the smooth handle." It was written by a man who was eminently a man of peace—who throughout his life would often say: " Peace is my passion." But to Jefferson there could be no peace without freedom. Indeed, to him there could never be true government, true education, true religion—without freedom. He and our people then, as in our own time, had felt oppression's " hand of force "—and they had boldly resisted.

When the shooting war began, Jefferson, as a member of the Continental Congress, was appointed to a committee to draft the Declaration of Independence. It was an eminent committee, with such members as John Adams and the venerable Benjamin Franklin. But Jefferson, just turned thirty-three, became its chairman; and his colleagues unanimously insisted that he should write the Great Declaration of 1776. Young as he was, said John Adams, he was the proper man to do it. He was remarkably learned in political theory, most capable in political action, but above all he had " the reputation of a masterly pen " that distinguished everything he wrote with a " peculiar felicity of expression."

In felicitous and imperishable prose the Declaration drafted by Jefferson, and approved by Congress on July 4, 1776, announced the birth of a new nation, listed the causes that brought it into being, and set forth the basic democratic philosophy that not only justified the embattled patriots of '76 but henceforth was to be the creed of all freedom-loving peoples who share its author's faith in human integrity.

In just a few words he encompassed the fundamental, inherent, unchangeable rights of man. Moral truths—as valid today as in 1776. Familiar words—yet ever-fresh, ever-inspiring. Never have they had so sharp an edge, so rich a meaning, as in our time when the whole free world has been put under siege by a Communist tyranny that daily becomes more powerful, more menacing.

> We hold these truths to be self-evident: that all men are created equal; that they are endowed by their Creator with certain inalienable rights; that among these are life, liberty, and the pursuit of happiness; that to secure these rights governments are instituted among men, deriving their just powers from the consent of the governed; that whenever

any form of government becomes destructive of these ends, it is the right of the people to alter or abolish it, and to institute new government, laying its foundation on such principles, and organizing its powers in such forms, as to them shall seem most likely to effect their safety and happiness.

Here was not just a manifesto converting colonies into a new nation, but a charter of freedom for all mankind. It voiced and gave new meaning to human aspirations when it proclaimed the primacy of individuals, possessing sacred and inviolable rights, and insisted that man was not made for the state but rather that the state was made by and for man. No longer were these principles the ideals held by a few philosophers. For the first time in history a people had made them the foundation of their government and their society.

And always these principles would be a standing challenge to tyranny—as they are today to the totalitarianism that reigns over such a large part of the world. Their continuing significance was very well expressed by Lincoln when he said: " The principles of Jefferson are the definitions and axioms of free society." They are " applicable to all men and all times, and . . . today, and in all coming days, . . . shall be a rebuke and a stumbling block to the very harbingers of reappearing tyranny and oppression."

In the Great Declaration Jefferson notably displayed his faculty of appealing to both the emotions and the intellect—" of leading the many by impressing their minds with happily concentrated propositions " of freedom. His words, so infused by faith and so pregnant with meaning, were greeted by the patriots of '76 with thunderous huzzas. Brave, glowing, pulse-quickening, they leaped over oceans and continents. Oppressed peoples all over the world looked to the United States—as ever since 1776 they have looked to the United States—as "the world's best hope," as the open door to life, liberty, and the pursuit of happiness. Men of liberal faith and expanded thought everywhere watched with grave concern our struggle for freedom. And it was a desperate struggle—eight years marked by grueling hardships and sacrifices. There was a price upon Jefferson's head—failure, he said, meant "hanging on a gallows as high as Haman's." Yet he fought on—in Congress, in the Virginia Assembly, as War Governor—to the final victory that secured independence.

Of all the Founding Fathers, Jefferson was most aware that the winning of independence was but the first chapter of a great epic, the great American story that is constantly evolving and never finished. It is one in which today our generation of Americans is writing another chapter. The War of Independence was but an introduction to a great, constructive social movement called the American Revolution. And that is a continuing revolution. For the Declaration of '76 on which it is based is a timeless appeal that the rights of all men there proclaimed be translated into everyday realities. That appeal rings down the years. It rings today—loud and clear.

Jefferson responded to that appeal for action, and responded magnificently, in the work of social reform that accompanied the war. By his deeds, the idealist, the penman of the Revolution, now gave point and effect to his faith in human integrity.

Three months after giving classic expression to that faith in the Great Declaration, he was back in Virginia to put into practice its inalienable rights. For him these were no "glittering generalities." He was tremendously in earnest. He passionately believed that the democratic philosophy could be applied—could be made to work—that its ideals could be made realities. And he was elated by the glorious opportunity afforded him to promote man's freedom and happiness; for our Revolution, as he said, " presented us with a [new] album on which we were free to write what we pleased." With Jeffersonian zeal he proceeded by his actions to write a noble chapter.

His program to transform the royal colony of Virginia into a democratic American commonwealth was carefully planned and most comprehensive. It embraced not only political freedom, but economic, religious, and intellectual freedom. He worked unceasingly for reforms by which, as he said, " every fibre would be eradicated of ancient or future aristocracy and a foundation laid for a government truly republican." He would remodel the whole legal structure " with a single eye to reason and the good of those for whose government it was framed." He would widen the suffrage, equalize legislative representation, abolish county oligarchies of appointive officials, separate church and state, insure freedom of conscience and the intellect, emancipate the slaves, provide a broad system of public education, and, among many other things, knock out feudal economic props sustaining a privileged hereditary aristocracy.

In general, he attacked special privilege, oppressions, and inequalities of every kind. At the same time, he opened wide the door of freedom and opportunity for all, and especially for individuals of merit and ability. For it was such individuals, he would often say, who form the only true aristocracy—" the aristocracy of virtue and talents."

From 1776 to 1779 he rallied and led the progressive

forces of Virginia in effecting this "Jeffersonian Revolution," as scholars are now calling it. He was forced to accept defeat, or postponement, on some of the legislative bills embodying his comprehensive program. But his victories were many, and most impressive. All in all he succeeded in effecting a bloodless social revolution in Virginia. In doing so, he gave a mighty impetus to the democratic movement throughout the new American republic.

Two of his far-reaching attempts to shape a better future for man claim our special attention, one a disappointing failure, and the other a glorious success.

Slavery, the perplexing and well-entrenched problem of human bondage, presented the supreme test to Jefferson's faith in human integrity. But this test was met with courage and consistency by the man who had proclaimed that all human beings are created equal and are endowed with inalienable rights to life, liberty, and the pursuit of happiness. Slavery, he acknowledged, was a tyrannical denial of this birthright of liberty. And not only did it cruelly degrade the Negro by denying him his birthright, it also undermined for all other men the very basis of human liberties: the conviction that freedom was a God-given gift to all mankind regardless of color or condition.

In his reform program he did succeed in prohibiting the further importation of slaves into Virginia. But he failed to win approval for his plan providing for a gradual elimination of slavery. The public mind was not up to it, he said. "Yet the day is not distant when it must bear it and adopt it, or worse will follow. Nothing is more certainly written in the book of fate than that these people are to be free." If some method of emancipation is not provided, he declared, " human nature must shudder at the prospect."

He derived some hope that the " sacred " cause of emancipation was gaining recruits from young men who were growing up in the newly-independent republic, sucking in " the principles of liberty, as it were, with their mother's milk." Such young men found in his writings an arsenal of arguments against slavery. But the grave problem continued to disturb him throughout his life. It caused him often, as he said, to " tremble for my country when I reflect that God is just; that his justice cannot sleep forever." And it led him to make this reflection on human nature in which hope struggled with disappointment: " What a stupendous, incomprehensible machine is man! who can endure toil, famine, stripes, imprisonment, and death itself in vindication of his own liberty, and the next moment . . . inflict on his fellow man a bondage, one hour of which is fraught with more misery than ages of that which he rose in rebellion to oppose." But he still ventured to hope that in time a God of justice, not by " his exterminating thunder," but " by diffusing light and liberality among their oppressors," would bring about " the deliverance of these, our suffering brethren."

Though he failed to abolish Negro slavery, he won a glorious victory for intellectual and spiritual liberty in his world-famous Virginia Statute for Religious Freedom. To win that victory Jefferson had to fight what he called the toughest and bitterest contest of his whole life, and in doing so he himself diffused a light and liberality that has a timeless significance.

He began the contest in the fall of 1776 by demanding the end of spiritual tyranny as embodied in a privileged, tax-supported state church. It took him and his colleagues three years to overthrow the Established Church of England, and win complete separation of church and state. But they had to wage an even longer struggle to enact his religious freedom bill. Many men opposed it as much too advanced for that day, much too radical and all-embracing. For it guaranteed, without any qualification, complete freedom of thought for all men whatever their belief or disbelief—comprehending, as Jefferson said, within the broad "mantle of its protection the Jew and the Gentile, the Christian and Mahometan, the Hindoo, and infidel of every denomination."

In urging its enactment, he argued most effectively against the folly of coercing men's minds and consciences. He lashed out at a "religious slavery" under which it was still legally possible to punish a man for unorthodox opinions by throwing him into prison or by burning him at the stake. Freedom of mind and conscience, he insisted, were natural rights of all men. For them we are answerable to no government but only to our God. "Reason and free inquiry are the only effectual agents against error, [and] will support the true religion by bringing every false one to . . . the test of their investigation." And why subject men's opinions to coercion? he asked.

> To produce uniformity. But is uniformity desirable? No more than of face and stature. Introduce the bed of Procrustes then, and, as there is danger that the large men may beat the small, make us all of a size, by lopping the former and stretching the latter. Difference of opinion is advantageous in religion [but] what has been the effect of coercion? To make one half the world fools, and the other half hypocrites. To support roguery and error all over the earth. . . .

> It is error alone which needs the support of government. Truth can stand by itself.

What Jefferson had to say about the tyranny of conformity has an eloquence and an urgency that forever insures him a high place among liberators of the human spirit. In his eighteenth-century world, in which state churches and enforced orthodoxy of belief generally prevailed, his bold words gave heart to all men who professed his faith in human integrity. And so they do today, in our twentieth-century world. For we are only too well aware of mounting pressures of various kinds to coerce men into a goose-stepping conformity of thought and action. There are the pressures exerted by totalitarians with their peculiar form of a state-church political religion which enchains man and deifies the state. But there are also coercive pressures exerted by business corporations with thier robot "Organization Man," by demagogs who would keep us captive to the prejudices of a dead past, by all too many fearful and timid Americans, woefully ignorant of the self-reliant individualism that is our Jeffersonian heritage.

When his religious freedom bill was finally enacted in 1786, with the aid of James Madison, Jefferson was our minister to France. He rejoiced that men of liberal faith in the Old World received it "with infinite approbation." It was an outstanding American contribution to the Enlightenment. Lord Bryce and other historians later praised it as marking the opening of a progressive epoch in human history. Jefferson himself considered it an achievement of such fundamental significance that he ranked it with the Declaration of Independence. From Paris he congratulated Madison, writing with pardonable pride:

> It is comfortable to see the standard of reason at length erected, after so many ages during which the human mind has been held in vassalage by kings, priests, and nobles; and it is honorable for us to have produced the first legislature who had the courage to declare that the reason of man may be trusted with the formation of his own opinions.

In those Revolutionary years the mature Jefferson had taken shape. He had revealed the essential qualities that distinguished the remainder of his life. He had eloquently expressed his basic faith in words that illuminate and inspire. And he had repeatedly affirmed that faith by his deeds. In those years he had placed his political and social philosophy on a solid foundation. All that came thereafter in his career was but superstructure.

We recall his services in Congress. His coinage system we still have. His famous report on the territories contained that vital principle of federal union—the equality of western states with the old thirteen states—which enabled the republic to expand as one nation to the Pacific. His attempt in 1784 to abolish slavery forever from all the territories from the Great Lakes to the Gulf of Mexico was defeated by only one vote. It was a dramatic event in our history, fraught with terrible significance. The fate of unborn millions, as Jefferson said, then depended upon the tongue of one congressman, and "Heaven was silent in that awful moment!" Yet he won a partial victory, since his prohibition of slavery was firmly placed in the Northwest Ordinance of 1787.

We recall his services as our minister to France. In Paris for five years he performed his official duties with distinction. Less known are the unofficial services he rendered the new nation by his "zeal to promote the general good of mankind by an interchange of useful things." He sent back home scientific apparatus, books, and useful information on many items ranging from the new phosphoric matches to pioneer work being done in navigating the skies and in applying mass-production methods to industry. He disagreed with his friend, the great scholar, Count de Buffon, who thought chemistry was but mere cookery. On the contrary, he insisted that this new science was "big with future discoveries for the utility . . . of the human race." He forced Buffon to alter his views on natural history; and he introduced in America new animals, new seeds, and new plants, believing that "the greatest service which can be rendered any country is to add a useful plant to its culture." He found time, also, to invent a portable copying-press, to design a phaeton, to make a map of his native state for his book, *Notes on Virginia,* and to draw up architectural plans for the beautiful state capitol at Richmond, which first introduced the neo-classical style in the new republic.

But in cultivating the arts and sciences, and in transmitting them to the New World, he was not blinded to the fate of man in the monarchical Old World. Appalled at the contrast between the wretched condition of the many and the privileged position of the few, he voiced his indignation at kings, priests, and nobles as "an abandoned confederacy against the happiness of the mass of the people." He himself, as well as the principles of his Declaration of 1776, was a pervasive influence on the movement to reform such conditions. When that movement boiled up in the violence and bloodshed of the French Revolution, he contrasted it with the bloodless reform accomplished in

America by the Constitution of 1787. Though he insisted that the new Constitution must be amended so as to insure the inalienable rights of individuals, he was proud indeed that America had " set the world a beautiful example of a government reformed by reason alone, without bloodshed."

We recall most vividly, perhaps, his great services in establishing the new national government on a sound and democratic basis. From 1790 to 1800, as Washington's Secretary of State, as party organizer and leader, and as Vice-President, he carried on a momentous struggle with Alexander Hamilton and his Federalists to determine whether America was to be an aristocratic or a democratic republic. It was a clear-cut issue, and one that will always exist, according to Jefferson. For all men, in all times, he said, are divided into two groups. There are those who do not have faith in man, who fear and distrust the people, and seek to draw all power into their own hands. And there are those who have faith in the people, and, while protecting minority rights, cherish majority rule as the cardinal principle of our republic.

It was a very bitter struggle, waged for a decade, by Jefferson's Democratic-Republicans against Hamilton's self-styled aristocracy of " the rich, the wise, and well-born." But it ended triumphantly in the people's political " Revolution of 1800," and as president for eight years Jefferson applied his democratic philosophy on a national scale, and on the whole with brilliant success.

When in 1809 he retired to Monticello after forty years in politics, he did not retire from public service. He continued to pursue those scholarly and utilitarian projects in which he had long delighted—devising new uses for the steam engine, studying the bones of the mammoth, and of the *Megalonyx Jeffersoni* he had discovered, inventing a hempbrake and a world-famous plow, experimenting with new crops, stock-breeding, and contour-plowing, collecting Indian vocabularies, proposing public libraries, or adding new books to his own library, the finest in America that was to become the nucleus of the Library of Congress.

In his old age as in his youth he welcomed innovations, whether scientific or social, that gave promise of improving the lot of mankind. For age and experience had only enlarged his progressive outlook and deepened his faith in human integrity.

It was a faith he still expressed in inspiring words, phrasing happily concentrated propositions of freedom. Again and again he would emphasize certain basic and timeless principles, as if to leave them as a legacy for the future. Each generation, he would repeatedly say, must be trusted to manage its own problems in its own way, for the earth belongs to the living, not the dead. Changing conditions in a changing world will force each generation to change its methods, since " laws and institutions must go hand in hand with the progress of the human mind . . . and keep pace with the times." But eternally unchangeable are man's inalienable rights and the selfsame democratic goals: man's freedom and happiness.

It was a faith he still expressed in deeds as well as words, one that sustained him in the arduous struggle he waged during the last decade of his life to further the cause of education. He fully, and passionately, subscribed to the view that what happens to American education will eventually happen to the American nation. He was insistent that, in his day, as in ours, the education we provide our children will determine our freedom and happiness, our individual and social well-being, our national security and, indeed, our national survival.

As a very old man he reopened a campaign begun forty years before, when as a young legislator he had fought might and main for this "sacred cause," but with only partial success. His great objective once again was a comprehensive system of tax-supported public education, from elementary schools for all children, to a university in which would be trained the only true aristocracy, "the aristocracy of virtue and talents." Once again he reiterated to complacent legislators that no nation can ever expect to be both ignorant and free; no nation can ever expect to live in ignorance with impunity. With all the zeal of his youth, the old gentleman pursued his "crusade against ignorance," that greatest enemy of man's freedom and happiness.

His educational plans were adopted by other states, and were so influential that they have been called "the charter of the American public school system." In his own Virginia, alas, he succeeded only with the university part of his broad system. But he considered this important enough to be the third of his contributions to mankind he wished inscribed on his tombstone.

He well deserved his title of "Father,"—not Founder, but "Father of the University of Virginia." He showed a tender parental concern for every detail—from getting money from penny-pinching legislators, planning his "broad, liberal, and *modern*" program of studies, to designing the beautiful buildings of his "academical village." It was a tremendous outpouring of energy, of love, of abiding faith. And it was done by an old man—a man, he said of himself, "with one foot in the grave and the other uplifted to follow it." This was a bit exaggerated. For the gallant and indomitable old gentleman did not rest from his incessant labors until just a few days before his death at the age of eighty-three, on July 4, 1826—the fiftieth anniversary of his Declaration of Independence.

He had won his last great victory. He had, most appropriately, closed " the last scenes of life by fashioning and fostering an establishment for the instruction of those who are to come after us. I hope its influence on their virtue, freedom, fame, and happiness will be salutary and permanent." He had surmounted all obstacles, all frustrations, and had opened his University—" this beautiful and hopeful institution," as he called it, " the hobby of my old age," where the education of youth will always be based " on the illimitable freedom of the human mind to explore and expose every subject susceptible of its contemplation."

It was his final testament, in both words and deeds, of his unfaltering faith in human integrity that had animated him through a long and fruitful life.

That faith had been the mainspring, the impelling motivation, of those three contributions he had inscribed on his tombstone. Each of them concerned freedom—the freedom essential to man's happiness. " Author of the American Declaration of Independence "—political freedom. " Of the Virginia Statute for Religious Freedom "—freedom of conscience. " And Father of the University of Virginia "—the basic intellectual freedom that safeguards all other freedoms.

Such are the words inscribed on his tombstone. But they are not just inscribed on the stone at Monticello. These inspiring and animating words are inscribed on the hearts and minds of Americans, and freedom-fighters the world over, who believe that the principles they represent are indeed " the definitions and axioms of free society . . . applicable to all men and all times," and who in our generation, by preserving and advancing man's freedom and happiness, would justify anew Thomas Jefferson's faith in human integrity.

II

# Individuality in the Work of Ralph Waldo Emerson

*by*

WILBERT SNOW

# *Individuality in the Work of Ralph Waldo Emerson*

EMERSON'S LIFE itself was a prime example of his individuality. As a youth he seemed to be living in a dream world. He was not excited by school life as students are supposed to be. Instead of entering into school life he stood apart, pondered and evaluated it. At Harvard, which in his day laid primary emphasis on the Greek and Roman classics, together with an allopathic dose of such books as Butler's *Analogy* and Paley's *Evidences of Christianity*, he stood in the lower third of his class. When men like Andrews Norton, father of Charles Eliot Norton, mentioned in their letters Emerson's education they almost invariably put the word " education " in quotation marks.

He apparently drifted into the ministry because it was the main business of Harvard in his day to train men for the Christian ministry, and because many in his own family looked to the ministry as a career. More than almost anyone I have known or read about, Emerson hated to be institutionalized, and he slid out of the ministry as soon as he could. He chose the administration of the sacrament of the Lord's Supper as his reason for quitting, but any other excuse might have served his purpose just as well. He preached a sermon in which he proved at length, by citing many authorities, that the first observance of the Lord's Supper was the Feast of the Passover which Christ, a Jew, attended with his Jewish disciples. As a Jewish feast, full of Oriental symbolism, he argued, it has no place in New England Protestant life, and Jesus never intended it to be a sacrament of the Church. He blamed St. Paul in his letter to the Corinthians as the real author of the rite, and questioned Paul's wisdom and authority. Emerson said he could no longer administer this sacrament, so must resign. You can imagine what a shock it was to his congregation to hear this thirty-two-year-old preacher emphasize the Jewishness of Jesus, proceed to attack a loved sacrament of the Church, and then go on to question the validity of St. Paul's position. Some of the church members recovered from the shock and urged their pastor to remain, but he would not. The truth is, he wanted to be his own man. His Aunt Mary Emerson, who probably had more influence on his thinking than anyone else, was determined that he should be an "original." He really loved the office of the clergy. In his journal for the 28th of August, 1838, he wrote,

> I dislike to be a clergyman and refuse to be one. Yet how rich a music would be to me a holy clergyman in my town. It seems to me he cannot be a man, quite and whole; yet how plain is the need of one, and how high, yes, highest, is the function. Here is a division of labor that I like not. A man must sacrifice his manhood for the social good. Something is wrong, I see not what.

He treats of the same subject in his poem "The Problem," whose first stanza goes,

> I like a church; I like a cowl:
> I love a prophet of the soul:
> And on my heart monastic aisles
> Fall like sweet strains, or pensive smiles:

Yet not for all his faith can see
Would I that cowlèd churchman be.

So he decided to embark on an uninstitutionalized career, and one can feel the joy in his verses, verses full of unnecessary exclamation points, as he leaves the ministry and writes:

GOOD BYE

Good-bye, proud world! I'm going home!
Thou art not my friend, and I'm not thine.
Long through the weary crowds I roam;
A river-bark on the ocean's brine,
Long I've been tossed like the driven foam;
But now, proud world! I'm going home.

Good-bye to Flattery's fawning face!
To Grandeur with his wise grimace;
To upstart Wealth's averted eye!
To supple Office, low and high;
To crowded halls, to court and street;
To frozen hearts and hasting feet;
To those who go, and those who come;
Good-bye, proud world! I'm going home.

I am going to my own hearthstone,
Bosomed in yon green hills alone,–
A secret nook in a pleasant land,
Whose groves the frolic fairies planned;
Where arches green, the livelong day,
Echo the blackbird's roundelay,
And vulgar feet have never trod
A spot that is sacred to thought and God.

O, when I am safe in my sylvan home,
I tread on the pride of Greece and Rome;
And when I am stretched beneath the pines,
Where the evening star so holy shines,

> I laugh at the lore and pride of man,
> At the sophist schools and the learned clan;
> For what are they all, in their high conceit,
> When man in the bush with God may meet?

The " secret nook in a pleasant land " he mentions in this poem was the little village of Concord. Here he enjoyed the pleasures of country life. Here he listened to the voice of Concord's little river, Musketaquid; and like Wordsworth, beneath this flow of sound, he heard the inner voice of the " silent stream that flows through water, rocks, air, rays of light, darkness, and through men and women as well." Hence the title of the poem, " Two Rivers." Here he followed the bee into the woods and came out of the wood with one of his finest poems, " The Humble Bee." Here he wrote his poem " Bacchus," finding a perfect analogy between the rich wines of Europe and the richer wines of New England landscape beauty. Here he kept a faithful journal of his reading and thinking, a journal which was originally dedicated to " The Spirit of America," when the conservative minds of Massachusetts thought the cultural spirit of America to be as rude as " the rude bridge that arched the flood."

Hawthorne tells us " it was good to meet him in the wood-paths, or sometimes in our avenue, with that pure intellectual gleam diffused about his presence like the garment of a shining one. His mind acted upon other minds of a certain constitution with wonderful magnetism, and drew many men upon long pilgrimages to speak to him face to face." Hawthorne adds that he was also visited by human " bats and owls and a whole host of night birds, which flapped their dusky wings against the gazer's eyes, and sometimes were mistaken for fowls of angelic feather."

He concludes, " Such delusions always hover nigh whenever a beacon fire of truth is kindled."

Emerson held long talks with Bronson Alcott, the irrepressible dreamer and educational reformer; went on long walks with Hawthorne, one of two days which covered thirty-nine miles, although these two men were never able to get close to each other in friendship.

He saw the greatness of Thoreau, his fellow townsman, as no one else did at the time. Some of the things he said about Thoreau on the occasion of his early death apply equally well to Emerson himself. For example, he wrote, " It requires rare decision to refuse all the accustomed patter and keep his solitary freedom at the cost of disappointing the natural expectations of his family and friends." Again in this eulogy he says, " He declined to give up his large ambition of knowledge and action for any narrow craft or profession, aiming at a much more comprehensive calling, the art of living well."

The art of living well was certainly in the mind of Emerson when he withdrew to Concord to live. Unlike Thoreau he could not accept single blessedness as his lot. And unlike Milton when he retired to Horton in Buckinghamshire, he had no rich father to fall back on. He had a living to make and a wife to support. Consequently he continued to fill a pulpit now and then, in spite of his refusal to become a professional preacher.

Before he finally settled in Concord, Emerson took a trip to Europe. He did this partly because of his sadness over the early death of Ellen, his first wife, and partly because of the lassitude and torpor and unsettled condition of his mind. He visited Landor, Wordsworth, Coleridge, and Carlyle, four living authors whose writings had made an impression on him. The result of this visit strengthened his faith in America. He expected more than he received from these immortals. Only one of them, Carlyle, made an indelible impression on him. And with Carlyle he entered into a friendship that lasted more than forty years. Carlyle always seemed to assume that he was the master and Emerson the pupil, and for a time Emerson did much to help the author of *Sartor Resartus* get his books published in America. But his over-all impression was that Americans had to visit Europe in order to get acquainted with and appreciate their own country. The visit to Europe did more than anything else to make him realize his own importance and the importance of democratic America. He exclaimed, " Can we never extract this tape-worm of Europe from the brain of our countrymen? " In his sailing ship on the way home, he sat in the cabin and wrote eight sentences which declare his creed; I give you six of them:

> A man contains all that is needful to his government within himself. He is made a law unto himself.
>
> All real good and evil that can befall him must be from himself. He only can do himself any good or any harm.
>
> Nothing can be given to him or taken from him but always there is a compensation.
>
> There is a correspondence between the human soul and everything that exists in the world; more properly, everything that is known to man.
>
> The purpose of life seems to be to acquaint man with himself.
>
> He is not to live to the future as described to him, but to live to the real future by living to the real present.

In these sentences can be found practically all the ideas that governed his later writings. No one before had ever made such an individualistic credo for man to live by. He was full of these ideas, and bursting with the desire to get them uttered. He was still the preacher, but a preacher unhampered by the restrictions of the clerical collar. He wanted man to realize his importance, and he wanted his beloved country to realize its greatness.

His first important utterance was an essay entitled "Nature." It is really a prose poem. In it he says that if the stars should come out once in a thousand years, men would record and recall their beauty and their mystery, and realize that they are God's gift to man. But things as awesome, as valuable and as surprising are with us every day. Only man has got into the habit of taking the sun, the stars, the moon, the rivers, the mountains, and the sea for granted. He has grown indifferent as to their wealth, their beauty, their meaning, and hence he exists in a state of merely living and partly living. Emerson in this essay gives us eyes to see, awakens us to the fact that the world was conceived in Beauty, and that Nature itself is "a flashing glance of Deity."

The essay is written in a striking epigrammatic style, a style designed for the listener more than for the reader. At the time Emerson was embarking on his career, the lyceum, the predecessor of the Chatauqua, was becoming an American institution. Lyceums were springing up all over the country. The change from farm life to industrial life had brought about a new leisure class. There were almost no adequate libraries. The people were hungry for learning and information, and the lyceum gave them music, drama, and lectures. Hence Emerson was embarking on his career at an auspicious moment in our history. Instead of a small parish of a few hundred souls, his parish included the thinking population of his country. And the young men, steeped in the dour, ugly, depressing gospel of Calvinism, listened eagerly to what this young, daring and independent lecturer had to say. This little book, "Nature," furnished an answer to their craving. They knew in their hearts that man was a creature of eternity, as he says magnificently in his poem "The Sphinx," but the eternity of John Calvin was a gloomy affair. They wanted something to match the hope, the crisp climate, the promise of American life, and this man furnished it. I cannot emphasize it better than to tell you that one of his booklets, "The Conduct of Life," sold out the entire edition in one day.

The lecture program on which he embarked was not only an inspiration to his readers; it revived the spirits of the man himself. It took away his apathy; it relieved him of his ill health; it gave him new and often rich contacts with many people. It convinced him that solitude, even in such an environment as Concord, was not enough to nourish his life. It taught him that man cannot afford to shut himself off from society, cannot afford to lose touch with his fellow men. His individuality did not carry him to the point of becoming a hermit. It is all right to say good-bye to the world, to go into the desert and rest awhile, as the gospel puts it, all right to go into the solitude where "man in the bush with God may meet," but too much solitude is as bad as too much society. He realized that man's stability on this planet is but balance, that the Aristotelian sense of proportion between the individual in solitude and the individual in society contains the secret of the good life.

He expressed this need of balance in his poem " Each and All," from which I quote a few lines:

> All are needed by each one;
> Nothing is fair or good alone.
> I thought the sparrow's note from heaven,
> Singing at dawn on the alder bough;
> I brought him home, in his nest, at even;
> He sings the song, but it cheers not now,
> For I did not bring home the river and sky;—
> He sang to my ear, they sang to my eye.

His next important utterance was his Phi Beta Kappa Address at Harvard entitled " The American Scholar," which has been called America's intellectual Declaration of Independence. This address has been called his most influential performance; hence we should take special note of it. When it was written in 1837 Emerson, age thirty-four, was at his peak. In May of that year he was thinking of the possibilities of the human race. He writes, " I see man is not what man should be. He is the treadle of a wheel. He is a tassel at the apron-string of society. . . ." " What answer is it to say it has always been so? The whole past is but one finite series in its infinite scope. Let me begin anew. Let me teach the finite to know its master. Let me ascend above my fate and work down upon the world."

These are brave words, but they show the temper of Emerson as he faced this Phi Beta Kappa audience. He wanted the scholars of America to write a fresh new chapter, saying,

We have listened too long to the courtly muses of Europe. The mind of this country, taught to aim at low objects, eats upon itself. There is no work for any but the decorous and the complaisant. Young men of the fairest promise, who begin life upon our shores, inflated by the mountain winds, shined upon by all the stars of God, find the earth below not in unison with these, but are hindered from action by the disgust which the principles on which business is managed inspire, and turn drudges, or die of disgust, some of them suicides. What is the remedy? They did not yet see, and thousands of young men as hopeful, now crowding to the barriers for the career, do not yet see, that if the single man plant himself indomitably on his instincts, and there abide, the huge world will come round to him. Patience,—patience; with the shades of all the good and great for company; and for solace the perspective of your own infinite life; and for work the study and the communication of principles, the making those instincts prevalent, the conversion of the world. Is it not the chief disgrace in the world, not to be an unit;—not to be reckoned one character;—not to yield that peculiar fruit which each man was created to bear, but to be reckoned in the gross, in the hundred, or the thousand, of the party, the section, to which we belong; and our opinion predicted geographically, as the north, or the south? Not so, brothers and friends,—please God, ours shall not be so. We will walk on our own feet; we will work with our own hands; we will speak our own minds. The study of letters shall no longer be a name for pity, for doubt, and for sensual indulgence. The dread of man and the love of man shall be a wall of defence and a wreath of joy around us all. A nation of men will for the first time exist, because each believes himself inspired by the Divine Soul which also inspires all men.

Nothing like this had ever been heard in America

before. The grim elders in the audience disapproved, but " the young men," one writer said, " went out from it as if a prophet had been proclaiming to them, 'Thus saith the Lord.' " The independent, individual Yankee is here raised from a material to a spiritual plane in breath-taking sentences. The Yankee preacher of unfettered idealism in this utterance took hold of the thinking young men of America and prepared them to face the nation's greatest crisis that was coming a few years later.

If " The American Scholar " was a triumph, his next great effort, " The Divinity School Address," delivered to the graduating class of Harvard Divinity School, was to him a disaster. The ideas in this address had already been expressed in " Nature," in " The American Scholar," and in some of his poems, especially in such lines as

> The word unto the prophet spoken
> Was writ in tables yet unbroken.

That is, Revelation is a continuing process. But in this case he was addressing himself to men preparing for the ministry, and his subject was religion, always a touchy matter. His journal, while he was preparing for this occasion, shows that he feared there would be repercussions. His fears were well grounded. But he felt deeply that the preachers in his day were superficial and unworthy of their exalted calling. In his journal of this period he writes:

> If I go into the churches in these days, I usually find the preacher, in proportion to his intelligence, to be cunning, so that the whole institution sounds hollow. . . . But in the days of the pilgrims and the Puritans the preachers were the victims of the same faith with which they whipped and persecuted other men, and their sermons are strong, imaginative, fervid, and every word a cube of stone.

He had the highest ideal of the preacher's calling, and wanted to arouse the young men going into the ministry out of their lethargy. He again says in his journal, " When I have as clear a sense as now that I am speaking simple truth, without any bias, any foreign interest in the matter, all railing, all unwillingness to hear, all danger of injury to the conscience, dwindle and disappear. I refer to the discourse, now growing under my eye, to the Divinity School."

Imagine the effect of such sentences as these on a group of theological students and professors:

> If a man is at heart just, then in so far is he God.
>
> It (religion) cannot be received at second hand.
>
> Jesus Christ saw with open eye the mystery of the soul. Alone in all history he estimated the greatness of man. . . . He saw that God incarnates himself in man and ever goes forth anew to take possession of his world. . . . He said, " I am divine. Through me God acts; through me, speaks. Would you see God, see me; or see thee, when thou also thinkest as I now think! "

Emerson was saying that God was in Christ, but only in the same way that he may be in any man who thinks as Christ thought, any man who is pure of soul.

He goes on,

> But what a distortion did his doctrine and his memory suffer in the same, in the next, and in the following ages! . . . He spoke of miracles; for he felt that man's life was a miracle, and all that man doth, and he knew that this daily miracle shines as the character ascends. But the word Miracle, as pronounced by Christian churches, gives a false impression; it is Monster. It is not one with the blowing clover and the falling rain. . . . Historical Chris-

> tianity has fallen into the error that corrupts all attempts to communicate religion . . . it is not a doctrine of the soul, but an exaggeration of the personal, the positive, the ritual. It dwells about the *person* of Jesus. The soul knows no persons. It invites every man to expand to the full circle of the universe and will have no preferences but those of spontaneous love. . . . And thus, *by his holy thoughts,* Jesus serves us, *and thus only.* . . . A true conversion, a true Christ, is now, as always, to be made by the reception of beautiful sentiments.

Thus did Emerson throw overboard the church doctrines of atonement, of regeneration through baptism, and all the rest of churchianity that had become sacred to believers. His audience heard him with dismay.

The elders could stand it no longer. They banished Emerson from Harvard, and he was *persona non grata* on the campus for over twenty years. He did say words of comfort at the close of this address. " All attempts to project a new Cultus seems to me vain. Rather let the breath of a new life be breathed by you through the forms already existing." But they refused to be comforted. He had called historical Christianity a dead faith, and men of influence and position denounced him in letters and in the public press. Emerson remained calm outwardly, but inwardly he was deeply disturbed, as his journal of the period indicates. He refused to argue the theological points he had raised, saying that all argumentation about such matters was useless and harmful. When he had recovered from the blow he wrote a poem which symbolically covered the entire controversy. It is entitled " Uriel " and is a poem purposely made " caviar to the general." It is named for Milton's archangel of the sun.

## URIEL

It fell in the ancient periods
Which the brooding soul surveys,
Or ever the wild Time coined itself
Into calendar months and days.

This was the lapse of Uriel,
Which in Paradise befell.
Once, among the Pleiads walking,
Seyd overheard the young gods talking;
And the treason, too long pent,
To his ears was evident.
The young deities discussed
Laws of form, and meter just,
Orb, quintessence, and sunbeams,
What subsisteth, and what seems.
One, with low tones that decide,
And doubt and reverend use defied,
With a look that solved the sphere,
And stirred the devils everywhere,
Gave his sentiment divine
Against the being of a line.
"Line in nature is not found;
Unit and universe are round;
In vain produced, all rays return;
Evil will bless, and ice will burn."
As Uriel spoke with piercing eye,
A shudder ran around the sky;
The stern old war gods shook their heads,
The seraphs frowned from myrtle-beds;
Seemed to the holy festival
The rash word boded ill to all;
The balance-beam of Fate was bent;
The bounds of good and ill were rent;

Strong Hades could not keep his own,
But all slid to confusion.

A sad self-knowledge, withering, fell
On the beauty of Uriel;
In heaven once eminent, the god
Withdrew, that hour, into his cloud;
Whether doomed to long gyration
In the sea of generation,
Or by knowledge grown too bright
To hit the nerve of feebler sight.
Straightway, a forgetting wind
Stole over the celestial kind,
And their lips the secret kept,
If in ashes the fire-seed slept.
But now and then, truth-speaking things
Shamed the angels' veiling wings;
And, shrilling from the solar course,
Or from fruit of chemic force,
Procession of a soul in matter,
Or the speeding change of water,
Or out of the good of evil born,
Came Uriel's voice of cherub scorn,
And a blush tinged the upper sky,
And the gods shook, they knew not why.

After Emerson " withdrew into his cloud," that is, after he was rejected by the divines of Harvard and its vicinity, he wrote what is generally regarded as his masterpiece. " Self-Reliance " was written when his mind was deeply agitated, and the agitation struck sparks in him that brought out many of his most memorable sayings. In this essay we find,

> To believe your own thought, to believe that what is true for you in your private heart is true for all men,—that is genius.

A man should learn to detect and watch that gleam of light which flashes across his mind from within, more than the lustre of the firmament of bards and sages.

[Works of genius] teach us to abide by our spontaneous impression with good-humored inflexibility, then, most, when the whole cry of voices is on the other side.

Trust thyself: every heart vibrates to that iron string.

Whoso would be a man must be a non-conformist.

Nothing is at last sacred but the integrity of your own mind.

My life is for itself and not for a spectacle.

What I must do is all that concerns me, not what people think.

It is easy in the world to live after the world's opinion; it is easy in solitude to live after our own; but the great man is he who, in the midst of the crowd, keeps with perfect sweetness the independence of solitude.

To be great is to be misunderstood.
But you may give your friends pain. Yes, but I cannot sell my liberty and my power, to save their sensibility.

Discontent is the want of self-reliance: it is infirmity of will.

These are only a few sentences from his remarkable essay, expressing his individuality, his self-dependence, his courageous convictions in unforgettable language.

There are spots in this essay where under the goad of his critics he seems to have gone too far. For example, he decries dependence on the historical past so violently that he is willing to "shove Jesus and Judas equally aside." Also "If I am the Devil's child I will live by the Devil."

Or " Travelling is a fool's Paradise," this when we know that it was his first European travel that brought him to appreciate the integrity of his own mind and the greatness of his native land. These sentences from " Self-Reliance " show how deeply he was affected by the criticism of his Divinity School Address, and how determined he was to go on in his own way regardless of the consequences.

Although Emerson called an institution merely the " lengthened shadow of a man," he did not want his own shadow to be darkened by echoes, imitators, and camp-followers. His test was uniqueness of individuality. In " Self-Reliance " he says, " When you have life in yourself, it is not by any known or accustomed way; you shall not discern the footprints of any other; you shall not see the face of man; you shall not hear any name;—the way, the thought, the good, shall be wholly strange and new." Again, " That which each can do best, none but his Maker can teach him." " It is only as man puts off all foreign support and stands alone that I see him to be strong and to prevail. He is weaker by every recruit to his banner." Late in his journal he writes:

> I have been writing and speaking what were once called novelties for twenty-five or thirty years, and have not now one disciple. Why? Not that what I said was not true, not that it has not found intelligent receivers; but because it did not go from any wish in me to bring men to me, but to themselves. I delight in driving them from me. What could I do if they came to me? They would interrupt and encumber me. This is my boast that I have no school follower. I should count it a measure of the impurity of insight, if it did not create independence.

It is not altogether true that he lacked disciples. It is true that his followers were not echoes of the Concord sage. They had absorbed his spirit too well to become " little Emersons." They were creators in their own right, but they were endued with his magnificent spirit. I shall mention three. First, there is Walt Whitman. Whitman began his career writing traditionally sentimental verses and stories. They were mediocre to an astonishing degree. Then he read and fell under the spirit of the only man he ever called *Master*. He must have read Emerson's essay " The Poet," an essay which called for a new poet for democratic America, one whose subject matter and form would be commensurate with the breadth of the continent, and whose vision would match the depth of Jefferson's Declaration. Whitman said, " I was simmering and Emerson brought me to a boil." Out of this boiling came *Leaves of Grass*, which the Master hailed as the greatest bit of wit and wisdom yet produced on this continent.

Then there is Emily Dickinson, whose poetry matched his in its epigrammatic power, and whose thought of man as a creature of eternity rather than a creature of time paralleled his own. Her poem beginning " I taste a liquor never brewed / from tankards scooped in pearl," treats the theme of Emerson's Bacchus with a woman's keen perspicacity, and with a power of imagery equal to his own.

Lastly there is Robert Frost, a poet who is trying to " find his place among the infinities " as Emerson did, a man who is perhaps more conscious of " the obscuration of the earth " than the Master, but whose Puritanical spirit and imaginative daring are part and parcel of the same New England tradition. Each of these three has gone his own way, but each one knew and absorbed the spirit of this bringer of light to materialistic America; and their work is richer because of him.

Nothing reveals the individuality of Emerson more strikingly than the attempts of his critics and commentators to label and classify him. Matthew Arnold said that he was a great teacher of life but not a philosopher because he made no system. John Dewey, on the other hand, says that he was a philosopher, assuring us that his " intuitive perception " was something beyond, something higher than a system of syllogistic reasoning, adding that intuitive perception plunges " deeper into the heart of things than cold reasoning ever could." Others say that he was the creator of wise sayings like the author of the Proverbs in the Bible, like the Greek Epictetus, or the Roman Marcus Aurelius, or the Frenchman La Rochefoucauld. His essays touch the periphery of each one of these classifications. But he refuses to be labeled, pigeon-holed, and classified. And here possibly more than anywhere else his uniqueness reveals itself. He was a bringer of light to a Calvinistic-darkened America. The light he shed came from his inner self, from his trust of what he calls the Oversoul. It had in it much of the neo-Platonism of Plotinus, much of the illumination of Emanuel Swedenborg, and some of the " inner light " of the Quakers. But the combined product was Emerson. These three influences working together in his mind and on his spirit issued forth in something all his own, something unique in the world of philosophy and religion,—something unclassifiable, to be sure, but something we all ought to recognize and be thankful for,—all in all the most germinal writer that has yet appeared in America.

III

# The Whole Individual: A Health View

*by*

MILTON ROSENBAUM

# *The Whole Individual: A Health View*

THE TITLE OF the Franklin Memorial lecture series for the current year is *The Growth of Self-Insight*—a title which could lead easily to philosophical and theological speculation. This I know, for when I first read the title I heard the tempting call from these august fields. But I am a physician; one who has spent his professional life dealing with those who are threatened by sickness, by pain and by death, and although it is possible and no doubt legitimate to speculate philosophically and theologically about these threats, it is another thing to be a witness to their presence and to report on what one has seen. You will understand, therefore, that I was glad when, in the course of discussions between myself and the sponsors of this lectureship, it was suggested that I might expand on the title "The Whole Individual: A Health View"; for here was a title leading me directly into the earthy realm of sickness and of health—a realm with which we are all, in spite of speculation and because of being alive, familiar.

Therefore, I decided to share with you those thoughts, reflections, and experiences which I have come to appreciate over the course of the years. It is because of my experience in the practice and the teaching of psychiatric medicine that I invite you to come with me into the clinics, wards, and research laboratories of a teaching hospital in a school of medicine where you will stand at the bedside of the sick. I will be your guide pointing out their fragmented, disintegrated, splintered individualities. You will soon see how the sick are deprived of "wholeness." Some by virtue of their sickness have lost this wholeness temporarily; there are others who in the course of development have never attained it and may end their lives without ever experiencing true health, namely, wholeness of being. But here a word of warning lest I lead you into an error all too commonly made and, I may add, an error which I and my colleagues are continuously on the alert to avoid. I refer to the error of judging wholeness in another person, sick or well, without taking into consideration one's own knowledge of oneself. In recent years in medicine as in physics it has been clearly shown that the nature of the observer cannot be ignored if the nature of the observed is to be understood. Hence, we shall keep in mind in our imaginary visit to the wards that we must constantly observe our own thoughts, feelings, emotions and attitudes, as we attempt to observe the sick; this we must do if we are to grasp fully the meaning of "the fragmented person" on the one hand, and "the whole person" on the other.

What does the term "whole person" mean? The answer will become evident in the course of my discussion; but I would like to say that it does *not* mean—in the sense that I propose to ascribe to it this evening—the same thing as the term "The Individual as a Whole," which refers to a particular view of the human person taken by a growing field of medicine, namely, psychosomatic medicine. It is true that this field of medicine has brought its salutary influence to bear on the need to recognize illness as an experience of the total being rather than as a derangement of the mind in isolation from the body or conversely of the body in isolation from the mind. But, as I have indicated, it is not with reference to this sense of " total " or " whole human being " that I intend to speak this evening. By " whole individual," I refer to that stage of psychological and physiological development of man which allows for meaningful interplay between the world-outside-and-the-self and that which we are wont to call the self's inner world. It is when this harmony of outer and inner worlds has occurred that the person has achieved wholeness in the sense that I intend to use this term this evening. It is at this stage of development that the person arrives at an awareness of self as a distinct and separate entity in the natural world of which he is a part. In other words, if a person's development has been successful, he will arrive at a stage when by virtue of meaningfully relating the outer and the inner worlds he *is* a whole being; and, furthermore, at this stage he is able to perceive and feel himself as such. I know that it will not surprise you to see how much anguish, misery, and suffering result from the failure of the person to become whole—from the failure to relate the outer to the inner world, from the failure to distinguish between events originating in one or the other world and from the failure to distinguish the self from those objects to which the self is related.

To clarify what I have just said, let us turn our attention to that phase of the person's development in which there is no differentiation or at best very little differentiation between self and the world other than self. Normally in early infancy, the infant does not differentiate stimuli originating within itself from those originating outside itself. To the infant, for example, the mothering person is not perceived as an object separate and distinct from the infant self. On the contrary the infant probably perceives the mother as a part of itself. In infancy, psychological wholeness is compatible with this truly and temporarily symbiotic or parasitic relationship. In the course of subsequent development, the infant gains the ability to distinguish between itself as a discrete object and other discrete objects to which the infant is in one way or another related. To express what I have just said in classical psychoanalytical terminology, I would say that the ego is being differentiated and formed insofar as that mechanism is developing in the personality (more precisely, in that part of the mental apparatus which can perceive stimuli arising from within as well as from without the person), so that ultimately the emotional needs of the organism can be gratified by the human objects in the person's environment. Furthermore, from a classical psychoanalytical point of view, one would say that object relationships so crucial to the development of the human being can occur only after the child has separated itself psychologically from the object to which it was originally attached. Yet I must emphasize that after separation and individuation has occurred the psychic apparatus still contains mental or psychic representatives of those objects that were meaningful in the individual's early development. That part of the mental apparatus called the super-ego and ego-ideal, or more commonly the conscience, is made up of such psychic representatives and memory traces of objects from the past. These internal and eternal monuments make each of us at one and the same time unique, different, and yet similar; encourage us to reach the heights of human performance and yet can plunge us into the depths of despair, misery and sickness. Wholeness can only be achieved when harmony exists in the psychic apparatus; but if one part of the psychic apparatus such as the super-ego and ego-ideal gains too much control or dominates the psychic apparatus in tyrannical fashion, then wholeness and health give way to fragmentation and illness.

Sometimes the child is blocked, hampered or hindered in its attempt to make this crucial psychological separation, and to the extent that it is thus impeded it becomes more vulnerable to illness of one or another form in its future life. You may well ask: "Why is this child blocked?" Because the mother or the mother figure has not been able, for any one or more of a wide variety of reasons, to endure the separation and consequently, for her own needs, has resisted, most frequently unbeknown to herself, the child's attempt to achieve this vital separation.

As an example, let me tell you about a young woman who in spite of reaching adulthood and marriage was never able to perceive herself as a unique, distinct, whole individual. On the contrary, she continuously perceived herself as a part of her own mother. The entire treatment of this patient was designed to free her from the image of herself as part of the continuum of her mother. No words of mine could describe as vividly the relationship between this patient and her mother as those used by the patient herself. I quote her words: "I am inside of mother and mother is inside of me." When this sort of relationship—this fusion of two beings rather than interaction between beings—persists beyond a critical stage of development, it is designated by a particular term: namely, symbiotic relationship. Since a symbiotic relationship is characteristic and normal during early infancy, perhaps the continuation of such a relationship might be labeled parasitic rather than symbiotic since usually the relationship continues mainly to fulfill the intense and pathological needs of one rather than the two. Recently child psychiatrists have described a severe type of childhood psychosis called " symbiotic psychosis," resulting from the continuation of the symbiotic or parasitic relationship and thus pointing to the origin of these illnesses in the failure of the infant to achieve independent existence and awareness of self as a whole being.

We have seen, albeit briefly, how crucial to " wholeness " is the event of separation from the mothering object. Now let us turn our attention to another form of derangement in the relationship between the inner self and the outside world—another impediment to wholeness. It is scarcely necessary for me to point out that in order for the person to be appropriately related to the world around him a variety of necessary conditions must be met. Of these conditions we will consider two which can be the seat of mental and emotional aberrations. One of the conditions is that there must be an adequate functioning of the receptor mechanisms, the inner system of sensory receptors and signal receivers, or to put it in other words, an adequate functioning of the in-put system. A second condition is that there must be an adequate source of signal senders and stimulators and these stimuli must be strong enough to penetrate the in-put system so as to arouse a reaction. We now know a good deal about the behavior problems that result from a defect in the in-put system. For example, it is known that if the functioning of this system is reduced below a critical level, usually by organic or structural brain disease or damage of one sort or another, serious consequences follow.

Recently the attention of investigators has turned to the interesting field of sensory deprivation and it is to this particular subject that I now wish to address myself. Autobiographical writings of explorers and shipwrecked individuals who underwent isolation for many days reveal that these people suffer from curious mental abnormalities. In his book called *Alone,* Admiral Richard E. Byrd describes how, after three months of being alone in the Antarctic, he realized that he was becoming severely depressed. He felt a strong need for "stimuli from the outside world" and yearned for "sounds, smells, voices and touch." Dr. Alain Bombard, in his book *The Voyage of the "Heretique"* describes his sail alone across the Atlantic Ocean for sixty-five days on a life-raft. He tells how he "wanted to have someone . . . who would confirm any impressions, or better still, argue about them. . . . I began to feel that . . . I would be incapable of discerning between the false and the true."

In addition to severe depressive feelings and anxiety states, other individuals under extreme stress and in conditions of extreme isolation have reported hallucinations and delusions. Captain Joshua Slocum, who sailed alone around the world in the latter part of the nineteenth century, describes an interesting experience during which he was restricted to his cabin because of illness. He suddenly saw a man, who at first he thought to be a pilot, take over the tiller. This man refused to take down the sails on request by Slocum but instead reassured him that he was a pilot and that he would safely navigate his ship through the storm. Later that night the pilot returned in a dream and reassured him that he would come whenever needed. During the remainder of the voyage, especially when there were gales, this apparition appeared to Captain Slocum several times. (The " pilot " is the projection of the psychic representative from the past—perhaps Slocum's father.)

Recently our attention has been focused on the phenomenon of " brain washing," about which interesting papers have appeared in psychiatric journals. Some authors paint a vivid and terrifying description of prisoner-of-war camps run by the Chinese communists during the Korean conflict and tell how the Chinese communists achieved their goal of making the men into a " group of isolates." In the words of one author: " The most important effect of the social isolation was the consequent emotional isolation which prevented a man from validating any of his previous attitudes and values through meaningful interaction with other men." One might say that each man was on his own life-raft separated and isolated from the other. After two or three months of such treatment, in addition to suffering from physical fatigue and illness, the prisoner usually became confused, " unable to clearly demarcate the boundaries of truth and fiction." He was depressed " frequently to the point of being suicidal " and sometimes experienced psychotic symptoms " such as auditory hallucinations."

In addition to the observations of explorers, adventurers and prisoners of war, there have been several research reports by psychiatrists and psychologists studying this phenomenon under experimental and laboratory conditions. One set of experiments was carried out in the laboratory of Dr. D. O. Hebb in Montreal. In this experiment healthy college students were placed in an environment in which there was a reduction of external stimuli to absolute low levels. The students were placed on comfortable beds in soundproof cubicles with their arms and hands enclosed in cardboard cuffs to minimize tactile stimuli. Their eyes were covered with translucent glasses permitting entry of light but abolishing all pattern and form of vision. After several hours, thinking became more progressively difficult, the need for external stimuli and bodily motion became intense, and those subjects who remained in the experimental cubicle longer than 72 hours usually developed hallucinations and delusions. Another set of experiments was conducted by Dr. John Lilly of the National Institutes of Mental Health, who suspended healthy human subjects in a tank of water, reducing to a minimum the intensity of physical stimuli they received. They too developed psychotic-like symptoms. Further evidence bearing on this same phenomenon was supplied recently by two investigators who reported the effects of sensory deprivation in a group of nine patients with poliomyelitis who required treatment in a tank-type respirator. After the patients had been in the tank from one to two days, mental abnormalities developed, characterized by visual and auditory hallucinations and delusions. Although there is still a question as to the neurological and psychological mechanisms involved in the development of the mental abnormalities following sensory isolation or deprivation, it is clear that the stability of man's mental state is contingent on adequate and meaningful stimulation from the outside world. Three hundred years ago, John Donne the poet pointed this out in his telling line: "No man is an island, entire of itself."

The production, by isolation, of mental abnormalities closely simulating psychotic states, especially those characterized by hallucinations, delusions and feelings of depression, is obviously of great interest to psychiatrists, especially those who believe strongly that many psychotic states, especially the schizophrenic disorders, are primarily due to psychological and emotional disturbances rather than to organic, structural, or biological disturbances in the brain or in any other region of the body. Of course, I realize that this is not the place to discuss the possible etiology of schizophrenia; yet, it is interesting to speculate about the possible cause of the sense of isolation so characteristic of the schizophrenic patient. Without becoming involved in theoretical issues, but rather with a view to supporting the thesis which I am trying to develop (namely, that the whole individual is in meaningful contact with the environment as well as with his personal or inner self) I would submit that the isolation of the schizophrenic patient which can be equated with his lack of wholeness is a manifestation of a disturbance of contact with the outside world, regardless of whether this disturbance is brought about by some biochemical disorder or physical defect within his central nervous system interfering with receiving, integrating, and synthesizing incoming signals, or from purely psychological forces within himself resulting in a withdrawal of meaningful emotional investment in environmental objects. Withdrawal from the outside world may also occur when the outer world is perceived as hostile or as one which offers little opportunity or even little or no hope of satisfying one's basic psychological needs. This unhappy state of affairs may account for some of the withdrawal and concomitant symptom formation both in some schizophrenic patients as well as in some of the mental disorders of old age or senility. The important point is that when the individual cannot stand to perceive the world outside as it really is, when he has to perceive that outer world in some false way to defend himself against inner unwholeness, the harmony of wholeness and health is lost.

Turning again to the clinic to illustrate the proposition that the sense of selfhood and of wholeness of the individual cannot take place in isolation but that, on the contrary, there has to be a proper feed-back between self and objects in order for health to be maintained, let me cite the effect of physical illness in diminishing the " wholeness " of the individual. In the face of physical illnesses, especially those which are acute in onset, certain types of emotional reactions occur which are virtually universal and which by and large are characterized by the phenomenon of a psychological regression to more childlike types of behavior. Perhaps the outstanding feature of this regression is the appearance of behavioral patterns which we as psychiatrists label narcissistic. It was Freud who described how in the face of a threat to one's physical or biological integrity such as occurs in acute physical illness, the person withdraws his emotional investment (object libido) from the outside, turning back this emotional energy (cathexis) into the self. This process, in which infantile attitudes are restored, can be seen as a tendency towards an anachronistic, more infantile and therefore less effective type of wholeness. In psychoanalytic language, we would say that there is a withdrawal of object cathexis and an increase in secondary narcissism. About a hundred years before Freud, Charles Lamb described the same phenomenon in a delightful essay called " The Convalescent," in which he tells with penetrating insight of his own emotional reactions to a bout of an acute physical illness. What better description is possible of the withdrawal, the retreat or regression to narcissism than the following words of Lamb:

> How sickness enlarges the dimensions of a man's self to himself. He is his own exclusive object. Supreme selfishness is inculcated in him as his only duty. It is the two tables of the law to him. He has nothing to think of but how to get well. What passes out of doors or within them so he hears not the jarring of them affects him not.

So again we see that even though the self or sense of self is " inflated " or " enlarged " as Lamb would say, the individual is no longer a whole person insofar as he has ceased to be related to his surroundings.

In our culture there is a premium placed on independence of action and thought. Popular opinion would favor the concept that the whole individual is one who is independent even to the point of being totally sufficient unto himself, having little or no need for others. Yet most of us, just like the ants and the bees, the birds and the mammals, know instinctively that we need one another. This basic need of one person to be fulfilled through another is an explicit or implicit fundamental tenet of the great religions, which state in one way or another that men need one another and should love one another. It is not as a philosopher or theologian that I make these references but rather as a physician and a psychiatrist who has observed that health is impaired both psychologically and physiologically when there is a rupture of the bond linking the individual to those objects in the outer world which are meaningful and important to him. It has long been known by psychiatrists that actual separation, threatened separation, or fantasied separation, are among the most important determinants of the onset and course of psychiatric illness. In recent years, we have learned that these same human experiences play a most important role also in the onset and the course of physical illness. I and my colleagues, as well as many other psychiatric and medical clinicians and investigators, have pointed out the importance of the role of separation and its emotional concomitants and consequences in the psychosomatic disorders. Dr. George Engel and his co-workers have emphasized the importance of such emotional events in the precipitation and course of physical illness of all types. I wish to make it clear that the experience of separation with its emotional sequelae does not of itself cause an illness, whether it be physical or mental, but acts as an important contributing factor to the onset and course of the illness. As a matter of fact, in few if in any illnesses is there a single cause; but rather there is a cluster of causes, in which certainly not the least significant are the emotional upheavals related to the experience of separation.

Until recent times, the traditional approach in medicine was to study the patient as an individual but the individual seen as a conglomerate of tissues and organs. With the introduction of the psychosomatic approach, again the patient was viewed as an individual; but even though the emphasis was now on the individual as a sick patient rather than as an accumulation of diseased organs or tissues, there continued to be a tendency to view the individual as an isolated object. However, if the patient is to be approached as a whole individual in contrast to an isolated individual, then he must be studied and treated as a part of an interacting system; namely, as a part of the group to which he belongs, the most important members of which group constitute the family. Since the main thesis of my presentation tonight is that the whole individual is not isolated either from his inner self or from the world outside him, it would follow that once the individual becomes isolated actually or psychologically from others he cannot remain healthy any more than an infant can remain healthy if left to itself. Furthermore, when treating physically ill patients who as individuals are isolated or not whole in the sense I have defined, the physician must attempt to survey the field in which the patient operates, since by so doing valuable clues leading to some of the factors producing the illness will be uncovered; that is to say, factors of isolation or of rupture between the inner and outer worlds, which spell illness.

Unfortunately, such an approach to the study and treatment of the sick patient is not the order of the day even in some of our best teaching hospitals. An example is the young woman whom I saw on the medical wards of our hospital just a few weeks ago. This young woman was admitted to the medical service because of severe vomiting and marked weight loss. On physical examination, she was found to have a large liver and laboratory test confirming the fact that there was marked impairment in liver functions. The immediate cause of the liver disease was the ingestion of large amounts of wine and vermouth together with an inadequate diet. I saw this young woman a few days after her second admission to the hospital. Her first admission occurred about a year before, when, after treatment in the hospital for a month during which she received no specific therapy but good general medical care, she was discharged as improved. The young medical house officer who presented this case to me felt that the patient's difficulty was related to her intense worry over her young son, who had suffered from an epileptic illness since early childhood. Certainly this illness of her only child was a cause for concern and worry; but she had managed, nevertheless, to remain in good physical health without excessive drinking until some two years ago, her son being at this stage of her history eleven years of age.

A brief interview with the patient brought out the fact that for the first three years of her marriage she lived with her mother-in-law and then moved into an apartment building next to her own mother, where she continued to live for the ensuing nine years. The reason for moving near her mother was that the mother had become a chronic cardiac invalid, requiring the daughter to spend most of her time in the mother's apartment caring for her. At the time of the onset of the daughter's illness, two important events took place in her life: (1) Her one close friend married and then moved to a distant city, the patient not having heard from her since. (2) At about the same time, the patient's father retired and subsequently spent all of his time at home, so that he began to take over the care of the invalided mother. Without belaboring the point, it seemed clear to me that the onset of the patient's illness was related to her separation from her friend (mother-substitute) and from her mother rather than to the worry over her sick child. While I was discussing with the patient her relationship with her mother, the patient remarked: "Girls are supposed to be close to mother." During the first hospital admission the patient undoubtedly was treated as an individual but actually she was not a "whole individual," as witnessed by her pathological need for her mother, for whom perhaps another might be substituted in the same way that in the treatment of a diabetic patient one substitutes insulin for the natural agent necessary for survival. The failure to achieve wholeness, it would be expected, would lead to a quick exacerbation of her symptoms once she had left the hospital, which provided an environment in which her needs could be met, even though the doctors treating her might have been unaware of the deficiency which was being made good by the hospital environment. Any mothering person such as a doctor, who enters this patient's life in a significant way at such a moment, be it in the most seemingly business-like guise, will inevitably become party to her current wholeness problem and must be aware of it to understand and help her.

I have used the patient as a clinical example to illustrate some of the theoretical points and issues I have raised and discussed. The use of patients as examples is in keeping with medical tradition; but now let me shift the focus of attention from the patient to the doctor and use him as our clinical example, to illustrate that aspect of the whole individual which has to do with perception of the inner self. To him let us apply the age-old injunction "Know thyself."

Recently, in one of my supervisory sessions with a third-year psychiatric resident, I listened to a story that cast considerable light on the part the doctor's attitude can play in determining his patient's acceptance of medical care. The physician told me, with a good deal of chagrin, about his treatment of a young alcoholic woman, which had been terminated by the patient after only four interviews. The resident first remarked that the woman had been physically unattractive, even though another psychiatrist had found her to be quite good-looking. The resident reported that in the first interview he had established a low fee since he felt that otherwise the patient would not continue therapy; but in the next few interviews, he recalled, he had spoken disapprovingly to the patient because of her drinking and promiscuous behavior. She failed to return for the fifth interview. It was clear that the patient had been in a difficult life situation, that she had sought help and support from the psychiatrist and that he had been apparently blind to her needs. As we talked further, the resident realized that he had probably been more attracted to this patient than he had thought. He then admitted that he was always attracted to such women. In struggling with his own feelings toward the patient he attempted to protect and defend himself by an overly moralistic attitude and in so doing unconsciously set the stage for early termination (originally denied by deliberately setting a low fee to be sure the patient would continue)—not for the patient's benefit, but for his own.

The doctor-patient relationship has been the subject of much discussion by medical men and particularly psychiatrists, but until quite recently discussion was concerned more with the patient's role than the physician's. The fact that this relationship is a reciprocal one was overlooked. However, it is to be remembered that just as a patient harbors unconscious, illogical attitudes towards his physician, so the doctor may have irrational attitudes toward the patient reflecting themselves in the doctor's treatment of the patient. In a sense one might see these as friction points between a particular patient and the wholeness or wholeness needs at that moment of the doctor. The young doctor especially has a kind of precarious wholeness in the clinical situation which is relatively strange to him.

It is axiomatic that all human beings continually attempt to defend themselves against anxiety, protect their self-esteem and gratify their basic instinctual and ego needs. Doctors, being human beings, do likewise. But for the physician it may become more difficult to handle these basic needs simply because he deals continually with anxiety-provoking situations and anxiety-laden patients. Is it any wonder, therefore, that his own anxiety is increased? The physician, more than anyone else dealing with human beings, must be aware of his own feelings and must be able to recognize the particular pattern of psychological defense with which he reacts in the face of mounting anxiety. The reason why it is so important for the physician to have this self-awareness is that the defense which helps him to reduce his anxiety may be disturbing or otherwise noxious to his patients. In the face of increasing anxiety one physician may react habitually with hostility, whereas another may react by becoming indifferent and withdrawn. Such behavioral responses on the part of the physician may evoke deep anxiety in the patient, destroying what little security he has by arousing conscious fears of desertion, abandonment and punishment.

As a safeguard against attitudes and behavior patterns which may be stressful to patients, the physician must ask himself again and again questions such as these: " Is what I am doing for this patient in the patient's best interest or my own? " " Am I protecting the patient or myself? " " Am I doing this to satisfy my need to be loved and admired? " " Am I doing this because I really wish to get rid of the patient," " Am I dropping this patient, or losing interest, or withdrawing from the patient because I really cannot help him any further, or because I am afraid of my feelings towards him or her? "

On one occasion a psychiatrist recommended hospitalization to a distant city for a patient whom he had been treating on an ambulatory basis because he " felt " the patient was too sick to continue treatment outside hospital. Fortunately, some honest, courageous introspection and soul-searching brought the psychiatrist to realize that he was afraid *of*, and not *for*, the patient.

The critical point is that although the doctor may be unaware of the underlying reasons for such a maneuver as the one I have cited and may believe that he is instituting the best medical or psychiatric treatment, the patient may become worse. To the patient, the doctor's action, whatever the motives behind it, can mean rejection and abandonment rather than rational therapy.

The doctor's job is to help restore the patient to health, which means wholeness. In certain instances the patient can be restored to wholeness only by first experiencing a relationship with the doctor that closely resembles a mother-infant relationship. However, if the doctor's own needs are such that they are being gratified by and through the patient then the relationship may turn into a symbiotic or parasitic one—in which case the patient cannot be restored to wholeness and to health. Therefore the more the doctor's own emotional and instinctual needs are satisfied in his personal life the more his patients are insured against a symbiotic or parasitic relationship. The incident of the young physician with the young woman who broke off treatment, which I cited earlier, resulted from the doctor's desperate attempt to avoid exploiting the patient because of the strong temptation to satisfy his own instinctual needs in his professional life rather than in his private life.

What I have said so far has demonstrated, I trust, why it is so important for the physician to know himself and in addition to look into himself. This, I can assure you, is more easily said than done. Most of my colleagues with whom I have discussed this subject agree that the doctor has to be in contact with his inner self, but the question is raised as to how this desideratum is to be achieved. Certainly the answer is not easy to formulate; but let me, nevertheless, attempt its rough formulation.

The main reason that psychiatrists practicing psychoanalysis and/or psychoanalytic psychotherapy undergo a personal psychoanalysis is to uncover their own blind spots, to gain self-knowledge and to become acquainted with their inner selves. Indeed one of the best indicators of a successful psychoanalysis is that the analyst continues the process of " self-analysis " for years to come. The process of becoming acquainted with our inner selves is a continuum rather than being confined to one specific period of time—such as that characterized by the period of psychoanalytic treatment.

Admitting all of the advantages accruing to the physician who undergoes a psychoanalysis, it would remain a ridiculous suggestion, simply by virtue of its impracticality, to advocate that every physician undergo an analysis. Are there then ways other than psychoanalysis by which to increase self-knowledge? I believe there are, provided there be strong motivation for augmenting the capacity for self-inspection. In the practice of medicine it would be hoped that such motivation would accrue from a conscious awareness of the importance of self-knowledge in enhancing the efficacy of the physician as a healer of the sick. To inculcate this " essential awareness " by stressing the incalculable importance of the doctor-patient relationship and thereby converting the " essential awareness " to a conscious commitment is, I believe, one of the most important tasks of the teacher of medicine. There is no doubt in my mind that the calibre of medical practice of the hospital intern or resident, of the surgeon or the internist, will be determined as much (if not more) by the skillful handling of the doctor-patient relationship as by the handling of the stethoscope or scalpel.

The criteria for wholeness vary with the demands made by the social role. Sufficient integration of inner and outer worlds consistent with adequacy in one field of work or in one mode of life may not provide adequate wholeness in another. When one makes the choice of medicine as a profession, he must realize that, as a doctor, the challenge of his outer world demands a deeper insight into his inner world for balance. When this is lacking he fails to be a whole person and may therefore seriously limit his functioning as a physician; not in every case, but particularly when the wholeness of the patient is pertinent to the patients' problem, as in the examples I have quoted.

Yet, we are obliged to accept the fact that there are numerous obstacles hindering those who are interested in developing by a conscious effort their powers of introspection. Our culture does not give high priority to those who incline to introspection which, all too frequently, is equated with passivity and what, one might ask, is more abhorred in our culture than passivity and what more revered than activity? So-called " Doers " are preferred to so-called "Thinkers." Need I ask who there is who has not praised the "go-getter" and pitied the "egghead"? In this regard I am certain that everyone here is familiar with two terms introduced into the psychiatric vocabulary by C. J. Jung: "introvert" and "extrovert." Is it not so that we Americans are inclined to think of the "introvert" as a sick, pathologically tainted, unfortunate creature contrasting with the healthy, strong, virile extrovert, the enviably American and therefore good individual? The type of introspection I am referring to is that which is a means to an end rather than an end in itself. If the introspection is ruminative and obsessive then it becomes pathological. Many reflective people are also men of action.

It will amuse you to know that having written the above lines indicating the advantage in our own culture of being an extrovert, my attention was called to the following quotation from a British periodical: "It was a bad thing to be an extrovert. The terms (that is to say, the terms: Introvert and Extrovert) had already shed the modifications and refinements with which their creator (Professor Jung) had provided them. An introvert was reserved, intellectual; an extrovert noisy, and insensitive, with a disposition to some form of crypto-Fascism." It would seem that the British condemn the extrovert and we in this country condemn the introvert; but of course all of us know what the grave-digger in Hamlet had to say about the people who inhabit England: ". . . there the men are as mad as he," and Hamlet was if nothing else an introvert!

In addition to these cultural pressures operating against self-examination, there are the internal, personal, intrapsychic forces hindering introspection and accurate self-perception. The very basic forces delineated in psychoanalytical theory are here involved since it is these forces leading to repression in the unconscious with consequent impairment of self-perception that militate against the conscious wish to enhance self-knowledge. And yet in spite of these formidable internal and external obstacles, I continue to believe in the possibility of developing better awareness of one's inner self with a view to becoming more mature and more whole. If only one would make the maximum effort to accept full-heartedly and fully consciously the importance of being whole not only for personal gain but also for the sake of others, the gains could be incalculably great.

To make this complete, it might be necessary only to recognize fully the useless pain, misery and destruction stemming from a lack of wholeness while at the same time to see no less fully the freedom and rewards of creativity which are the fruits of health or wholeness. I believe that if this destruction on the one hand and creativity on the other were clearly perceived, then the necessary motivation would be provided. Once the motivation has been instituted, there would be numerous ways by which to deepen and broaden self-awareness. For example, so simple a procedure as the allocation of some time during the day in which to question one's own proclaimed intentions with a view to eliminating self-deceit would certainly help one to proceed in the direction of wholeness. Let me throw out one useful hint: when there is *absolute* certainty that one's intentions are of the highest order, this in itself can be taken as a signal to look further and to find self-deceit. Perhaps no less useful than the above suggestion would be to choose some person with whom one tends continuously to agree or disagree with passion and then to attempt to develop a strong argument in opposition to one's own position. If this were done, while attempting to discern in one's own past the duplication of a passion and the difficulty in seeing another point of view, one might discover a repetitive pattern of behavior, and whenever there is repetitive behavior there is absence of freedom stemming from absence of wholeness.

Needless to say, these hints are nothing more than passing remarks since it would take at least another complete lecture to develop systematically the methodology which I am indicating. However, before leaving this particular point, I must point out the self-awareness that can be gained through the arts; the artist, I take it, is one who sees more deeply and more clearly than less gifted mortals and by borrowing, so to speak, his vision—that is to say, the works created by him—one can hope to see more deeply and more clearly than oneself.

In closing, I would like to quote a recent statement by Mr. Stringfellow Barr, the noted educator and scholar. Mr. Barr writes: ". . . the soul of man is the destined meeting place of the knowledge that comes to us from the world of matter and the knowledge we get by looking inward. It is a bridge between these two worlds." And this thesis, namely, that it is such a meeting place and such a bridge, "was already old when Plato stated it." The bridge must be whole; the meeting place must not be divided. To this thesis experienced by me in the clinic, supported by research and hallowed by time, it has been my purpose to introduce you.

IV

# Goethe's Conception of Individuality and Personality

*by*

HAROLD A. BASILIUS

# *Goethe's Conception of Individuality and Personality*

philosophy is verbal rubble
  amidst its casual circumstance
gleaming acres gleaned to stubble
  ambivalent inheritance
*Vermächtnis ist die Zeit*
  demoniacally feministic time
*blühende zu Ewigkeit*
  eternally enhancing given rime
whose any linguistic token
  polarity transcending
temporally remains unbroken
  o rarity unending
concatenate and quite unspoken

*Chester F. Kuhn*

## I

ROUGHLY A DECADE ago, the bicentennial of Goethe's birth in Frankfurt am Main in 1749 was celebrated throughout the world. The occasion added still another enormous layer of reinterpretations and reassessments to the already formidable mountain of Goethe research. The bicentennial observance was particularly productive in the U. S. A., where a series of Goethe festivals in all major American centers, including Detroit, culminated in the week-long International Convocation in Aspen, Colorado.[1]

"Goethe und kein Ende"—no end to Goethe—a parody, published in *Books Abroad,* of Goethe's own essay on Shakespeare ("Shakespeare und kein Ende"—"Shakespeare ad Infinitum") epitomizes our frustration in the face of the prodigious documentation of the life and the works of Johann Wolfgang Goethe, who died only a little more than 125 years ago. The so-called Weimar Edition (1887-1912) of his collected works alone embraces 133 octavo volumes, and the scholarship concerning him runs to tens of thousands of books, monographs, and articles.

I should like, in this connection, to mention a fact I am fond of embroidering for my students. As you might expect, there are many extensive biographies of Goethe in many languages. The best, in my considered judgment, is *Goethe—The History of a Man* (New York, 1928), by Emil Ludwig, the well-known author of many other best-selling books. The story has it that, when Ludwig undertook to write a Goethe biography, he knew little more about Goethe than the run-of-the-mine educated German. Mr. Ludwig decided, therefore, to acquire the best informed opinion about Goethe. He did this by retaining the services of a dozen and a half young Ph. D.'s who had just come from the Goethe seminars of several leading German universities. These young Ph. D.'s wrote careful and detailed abstracts of the tons of the most up-to-date Goethe scholarship and were well paid for their services by Mr. Ludwig. By studying these abstracts and proceeding from this study to reading and rereading Goethe himself, Emil Ludwig prepared himself for writing the biography. The point of the story is, of course, the realization that only in this way could a really good biography of Goethe be written. Emil Ludwig first absorbed Goethe himself and then the almost insurmountable scholarship about Goethe. These materials he then reconstituted imaginatively and finally put his trained and talented pen to paper to produce a first-rate interpretative biography of Goethe.

The question naturally arises: Then why still another interpretation of Goethe in the 1960 Franklin Memorial Lectures in Human Relations? The answer is simple, clear, and compelling. There is probably no comparable personality in western history to whom the problem and question of the self was so central as it was to Goethe.

Goethe was a yea-sayer, to use Nietzsche's beautiful Biblical phrase: that is, Goethe was an affirmer of life and of the dignity and central importance of the individual. And he was this at a time when the nascent evidence of science, as we understand that term, began to suggest quite unmistakably that the brave new world of the nineteenth and twentieth centuries would be compelled to think and feel in terms of controlling material and mechanistic forces, the impersonal deterministic pointer readings of scientific instruments, as opposed to the will, the imagination, and the ethical aspirations of human individualities.

"Mechanization is gradually taking over, and this torments and frightens me," Goethe has one of his female characters say in *Wilhelm Meister's Journeyings.* "It approaches ominously like a storm, slowly, slowly; but it has taken its direction, and it will come and strike." [2]

"Microscopes and telescopes," he says elsewhere, "confuse basic human senses." [3]

To Riemer, one of his confidants, Goethe said (May 10, 1806): "Former ages thought in terms of images, whereas we moderns have concepts. Formerly the guiding ideas of life presented themselves in concrete visual form as divinities, whereas today they are conceptualized. The ancients excelled in creation; our own strength lies rather in destruction, in analysis." [4]

Despite such concerns and sentiments, however, Goethe also said: " However it be, I find life good." [5]

And the ringing affirmation and optimism of Lynceus, the Tower Keeper, in *Faust* are unmistakable:

> Zum Sehen geboren,
> Zum Schauen bestellt,
> Dem Turme geschworen,
> Gefällt mir die Welt.
>
> For seeing I'm born
> And appointed for sight,
> To the tower I'm sworn
> And the world's my delight.[6]

Karl Jaspers summed the matter up with the succinct statement: " Whenever Goethe is under consideration, personality is involved." [7]

Finally, Goethe is that most tantalizing combination of human individual, poet, philosopher, and scientist, who beckons us continuously and irresistibly, though he actually belongs to a golden age now irrevocably gone. For in our world, there are no philosophers, and philosophy itself exists only as an academic discipline and as a higher stratum of genteel journalism. We make persistent and frenetic, but quite unsuccessful, efforts to rehabilitate the poet, indeed, all creative artists; but poets like philosophers we are quite surely convinced, belong to a time beyond recall. Alas, even our faith in science and in scientists is threatened and wavers as a result of the evidence supporting theories of indeterminacy and relativity.

The Great God Pan is, indeed, dead!—to cite another of Nietzsche's grandiose phrases.

Goethe seems, however, to have had a secret. Barker Fairley, the Canadian scholar, describes him as being "Protean" and "chameleon-like." [8] Though Goethe belongs to the past, he nevertheless lived on the threshold of our own age. Unlike Emerson, Goethe did not conceive of Europe's poetry as being that of the "courtly muses." The poetry of the immediate present and future interested him much more. Nor was he exclusively the child of the fashionable Enlightenment of his day. The warm expansiveness of nascent romanticism was much more attractive to him. He succeeded in making his mark as a marvellous modern combination of human individual, scientist, philosopher, and poet.[9] For that reason, he "still draws us on," to quote his own winged word from *Faust* (line 12110) regarding the irresistible attraction of *Das Ewig-Weibliche.* ("The Ever-Womanly" or "The Woman-Soul," as the phrase has been variously translated.)

Only recently Stanley Kunitz wrote an exciting piece of dialog which strongly reminded me of Goethe's secret:

> POET: There would be no poems if poets did not have boldness, compulsions, cunning, science and luck.
>
> YOUNG MAN: Science seems a strange word for a poet to use in that context.
>
> POET: Why? The mind of the scientist, exploring space and matter, is closely related to the mind of the poet, whose task is to explore inner space and the reality of things. Like the scientist the poet is enchanted with an expanding universe of knowledge; but he keeps insisting that the new data must be incorporated into a moral universe that poetry originally created as myth and is perpetually in the process

> of re-creating. "After such knowledge, what forgiveness?" asked Eliot. Poets who blindly fight science are ignoring their commitment to the human ultimate. Ideally the mind of the poet is pulled in two ways at once; in one aspect, to the purity of the precision of mathematics; in the other, to the purity of the violence of love.[10]

Only a poet such as Kunitz could, I suppose, really express this complementary relationship between poet and scientist. And it is the remarkable combination of scientist and poet in a single personality, such as Goethe, that gives Anglo-Americans difficulty, for that kind of combination seems too incredibly mysterious; and anything essentially mysterious must be rejected on the grounds that the mysterious is the mystical, and the mystical is intolerable in our brave new world. To combine poet and scientist would be like combining Arthur Koestler's yogi and commissar in a single personality. Despite the fact that all totalitarian societies have done precisely that, we Anglo-Americans persist in denying the possibility.

Goethe's secret can be described and even defined to some extent by observing that he is a remarkable combination of the three kinds of history delineated by Friedrich Nietzsche in *The Use and Abuse of History* (1874).[11] He is the type of *monumental history* which provides men of action and power with examples. He exemplifies the type of *antiquarian history* required by men of conservative and reverent nature who need to understand their antecedents. Finally, Goethe personifies the type of *critical history* for men of action who require criteria whereby they can destroy the past for the purpose of building the future.

"Goethe [was]," as Nietzsche remarked, "not a German event, but a European one." [12] In today's language, Goethe was a universal event. We want to know his secret, first, just to know it, but second, because we persist in believing that, knowing it, we may be able to emulate it.

Karl Jaspers said as recently as 1948 that Goethe " stands so vividly before us from childhood to old age, as though we had encountered him personally throughout all phases of his life." [13]

Jaspers' opinion is shared by others, as a few examples will readily show. Among British writers, Thomas Carlyle's and Sir Walter Scott's great admiration for Goethe need no elaboration. The Frenchman André Gide has said: " I owe more (to Goethe) than to anyone else, perhaps more than to all others combined." [14] Of the German-speaking commentators, the views of Friedrich Nietzsche, Sigmund Freud, Franz Kafka, Karl Jaspers, Carl Jung, and Thomas Mann, to mention only a few, are too well known to require documentation here, except perhaps to emphasize that, whereas Anglo-American opinion of Goethe rests almost exclusively on the writings of the young Goethe, the Romantic and revolutionary Stormer and Stresser of the 1770's, Niezsche discovered, as it were, the mature or old Goethe and emphasized his spoken thoughts and sayings, remarking that the *Conversations with Eckermann* are more important and " greater " than *Faust*, an orientation which Thomas Mann also followed in his magnificent Goethe novel, *Lotte in Weimar: The Beloved Returns* (1949).

By marked contrast, a long and distinguished line of Anglo-American critics have repeatedly expressed reservations about Goethe, frequently on the moral grounds of Puritanism.[15] Emerson's phrase, " the velvet life," and

Calvin Thomas' "fleshly-mental" express the coloration of the prevailing attitude. The list includes, among others, Henry Wadsworth Longfellow, T. S. Eliot and George Santayana.

In 1929, T. S. Eliot said that "Goethe is at present in eclipse." [16] Karl Shapiro may very well have provided the clue to Eliot's dislike of Goethe in his very recent observation that "Eliot shows a positive hatred for originality, and in fact condemns it in every manifestation; originality is irresponsible freedom to him." [17] And if Goethe was anything, he was original to thepoint of being unique.

Ellis Roberts, a British observer, wrote in 1930: "For Goethe, most modern men, unless they are Germans, have a positive distaste." [18]

One of the notable exceptions to the prevailing Anglo-American disavowal of Goethe is Ludwig Lewisohn, whose two-volume *Goethe—The Story of a Man* (New York, 1949) has become a standard work.

"Had we but small groups of [Goethe's] sayings," Lewisohn asserts, "as we have of certain founders of religion, but scattered *logia*, pronouncements and parables, mankind would still be assured of the presence on earth of an exemplary life, not in the sense of entire virtue, but in the sense of all-inclusiveness, in the sense of that life's being the symbol of all human life." [19]

Barker Fairley says much the same in his several books about Goethe, only in greater detail and with particular reference to the relation between Goethe and his writings. And it is Fairley who continuously also stresses the contemporaneity of Goethe.[20]

The late George Santayana's judgment of Goethe may, however, be regarded as representative of the prevailing

Anglo-American view. It is also the most comprehensive statement and has quasi-official sanction, inasmuch as Santayana's book *Egotism in German Philosophy* was first published in Britain in 1916 and republished in New York in 1940, publication coinciding in both instances with the two great wars of our century. It " passed for a war-book," says Santayana, and was, indeed, written with " my sympathies warmly engaged upon the anti-German side." [21]

In another context (a book called *Three Philosophical Poets*), Santayana wrote: " Romanticism . . . is an attitude often found in English poetry, and characteristic of German philosophy. It was adopted by Emerson and ought to be sympathetic to Americans; for it expresses the self-trust of world-building youth, and mystical faith in will and action. The greatest monument to this romanticism is Goethe's *Faust*."

Santayana devoted one of the three essays in this book to Goethe as being the great representative of romanticism. A series of brief quotations from this Goethe essay will illustrate a certain ambivalence on Santayana's part, on the whole, however, an ultimate considered rejection of Goethe. " Goethe was the wisest of mankind; too wise, perhaps, to be a philosopher in the technical sense, or to try to harness this wide world in a brain-spun terminology." But to Goethe, he continues, " The worth of life lies in pursuing; therefore, everything is worth pursuing, and nothing brings satisfaction—save this endless destiny itself."

In Santayana's opinion, *Faust* " is the drama of a philosophical adventure; a rebellion against convention; a flight to nature, to tenderness, to beauty; and then a return to convention again, with a feeling that nature, tenderness, and beauty, unless found there, will not be found at all."

Santayana concludes: "The place in the moral world of Goethe's *Faust* as a whole is just the place the opening scene gave it in the beginning. It fills more space, it touches more historical and poetic matters; but its centre is the old centre, and its result the old result. It remains romantic in its pictures and its philosophy." [22]

Thus, Goethe has been consistently rejected by representative Americans and Englishmen, either because he was believed to be amoral or immoral, or because he was a romantic in the sense that he put a higher premium on the maximum development of individual human personality than on the attainment by human beings of certain socially approved goals.

The ironic paradox of this judgment and attitude is, as Santayana has said, that Goethe's attitude "ought to be sympathetic to Americans, for it expresses the self-trust of world-building youth, and mystical faith in will and action."

Goethe's expansiveness is just as democratic in an American sense, as his tolerance of irreconcilable and mutually exclusive opposites. It is important to keep in mind, however, that the ambivalent attitude which accompanies and results from that kind of tolerance is the unpardonable sin in the minds of social reactionaries and some schoolmasters. Such persons cannot tolerate an attitude of both-and. Their judgments must always be based on either-or. Hence, they find much of Goethe unacceptable, and they rationalize their judgment on the grounds that Goethe was immoral, or in the jargon of our day, subversive. Goethe is too strong and dangerous a dose for tender youth, they say, and the elders who say this will not read him either.

Goethe's pragmatic insistence on the necessity of combining thinking with doing anticipates John Dewey by better than fifty years, and Dewey's pragmatism is now generally regarded as the single great contribution to philosophy by an American.

American experientialism might well have taken as its motto that famous line, spoken by the Lord God to Mephisto in *Faust* (l. 317):

> Es irrt der Mensch, solang er strebt.
>
> Man's bound to err the while he strives.

Finally, can there be a sentiment more American than that magnificent couplet in *Faust* (ll. 2038-9) spoken by Mephisto to the student?

> Grau, teurer Freund, ist alle Theorie.
> und grün des Lebens goldner Baum.
>
> Gray, my good friend, are all your theories,
> And green alone Life's golden tree!

I personally believe, however, that the language barrier has been and continues to be a great deterrent to any American appreciation of Goethe. Not too many Americans read German well and easily; and imaginative writing, particularly lyric poetry, is often very difficult in any language. The English translations of Goethe are, on the whole, not distinguished; and the language of many of these translations is hopelessly and often ludicrously dated. I agree completely with Hermann Weigand's observation that "most (English) translations of Goethe, however carefully done, make him sound like a third-rate Victorian." [23]

## II

On our campus and in this auditorium, Robert Maynard Hutchins recently remarked again the American inclination to confuse ideas and things with their names. Terms such as "self," "personality," "individuality," terms basic to this lecture series, are good illustrations. We all incline to think, or rather to feel, that we know positively and agree on whatever it is that the term "personality" designates. Nothing could be farther from the fact.

A Roosevelt University sociologist observed as recently as 1958 that, although the individual behavioral sciences (anthropology, sociology, psychoanalysis, psychology) have cross-fertilized and enriched each other in the study of personality and culture, "areas of disagreement [still] remain." [24] The disagreement revolves about the old question of whether the culture is the prime determinant of individual personality, or vice versa.

Thus, we find Professor Clyde Kluckhohn saying:

> Which of the many courses of behavior within an individual's physical and mental capacities he characteristically takes is determined in part by culture. . . . When a person has surrendered much of his physiological autonomy to cultural control, when he behaves most of the time as others do in following cultural routines, he is then socialized. Those who retain too great a measure of independence are necessarily confined in the asylum or jail.

But a little farther on, Kluckhohn observes that "emphasis must be laid—because of the findings of psychoanalysis, anthropology, and the psychology of learning—upon human potentialities. . . . One of the wise things which Reinhold Niebuhr says in *The Nature and Destiny of Man* is that the contemporary world overestimates the powers of the 'collective will' and underestimates those of the individual will." [25]

This central importance of the individual will, as opposed to the collective will of social or political organization, was stressed in recent days by Dr. Henry Wriston, formerly president of Brown University and now president of the American Assembly at Columbia, and also chairman of President Eisenhower's National Goals Commission. The Commission has been charged with the task of defining the great issues of this generation and charting a course for dealing with them. In opening the deliberations of the Commission in New York last month, Dr. Wriston observed that there are two great issues dominant in America today. One, he said, is the place of the individual and his development in this complex world. The other is how to improve and strengthen the democratic process. The two fit together, he believes, for without individual people, there is no social growth.[26]

Obviously, one should be careful to define one's term when discussing personality. Louis Sullivan's grandiose rhetoric comes to mind here:

> Heard and seen by all stands the word PERSONALITY, in solitary and unique grandeur. Heard and seen by all stands the word *Personality,* eminent, respectable, much admired.
>
> Heard and seen by all in the crowd it calls together, and through which it deftly wanders like a shrewd hunch-back, the word *personality,* now a dwarf, grimaces salaciously.
>
> And now it is a word on fire; a tiger in the jungle; a python hanging from the limb, very still.[27]

To keep our discussion clear and cogent, we must pause

to consider whether or not the terms "personality" and "self" have the same referents today as they did in Goethe's time.

The climate of our day is one of crisis, and the President's National Goals Commission is obviously thinking and talking in crisis terms. Goethe's age, that of the late eighteenth-century Enlightenment, was also "An Age of Crisis." Indeed, that is the very title of an imposing book, by Professor Lester G. Crocker, published within the last several months. The subtitle reads "Man and World in Eighteenth-Century French Thought."

Crocker documents the thesis that underlying the Enlightenment world-view was the proposition that man is by nature good. Eighteenth-century thinkers, generally, believed that there is "a universal human nature which is prior—logically or historically—to society," and that "this fund of basic universality remains indestructible in the social state." This universal human nature was held to be "good" in the eighteenth century, and the term "implies the notion of 'non-egoistic,' of motivation by concern for others, or for the welfare of the community."[28]

Crocker then makes the point that opinion today has moved away markedly from the prevailing cultural relativism of yesterday and coincides much more closely with the views held in the eighteenth century. To corroborate his judgment, he cites Erich Fromm (a psychiatrist-philosopher), Noah Kramer (an archeologist), and Clyde Kluckhohn (an anthropologist).[28]

In view of the climate of eighteenth-century thought regarding the universal goodness of the universe and of man, it is not surprising to observe that the problem of the fully developed personality was central to Goethe's philosophical interest, just as he regarded the representation of man as the acme of the plastic arts. And it is precisely this concern with the self and its development, this basic concern with the growth of self-insight, which makes Goethe so contemporary and, if I may say so, so American.

## III

Goethe's writings and recorded conversations are replete with observations concerning the self, the importance of the development of the self, and the ways in which development of the self can and must be done. Indeed, he gave wings to the word " personality " in that famous quatrain from " Suleika " in the *West-Easterly Divan*:

> Volk und Knecht und Überwinder,
> Sie gestehn zu jeder Zeit:
> Höchstes Glück der Erdenkinder
> Sei nur die Persönlichkeit.
>
> Folk and slave and subjugator
> Will admit it readily;
> Children of earth have no boons greater
> Than their personality.[29]

As a matter of fact, Goethe devoted all or most of three major works to the problem of the development of the self, viz., the novel *The Elective Affinities* (*Die Wahlverwandtschaften*), the lyric drama *Faust,* and the Wilhelm Meister novels, *Wilhelm Meister's Apprenticeship* (*Wilhelm Meisters Lehrjahre*) and *Wilhelm Meister's Journeyings* (*Wilhelm Meisters Wanderjahre.*)

Indeed, the Meister novels are the prototype of that literary *genre* called the *Bildungsroman,* viz., the novel of personal development or of the plastic molding of character, which German literature claims as its most unique and characteristic literary achievement. Every significant German man of letters has, since Goethe's Meister novels, tried his hand at this genre. Incidentally, the Meister novels revolve about an educational theme still very much alive today in the U. S. A. The theme of the first novel, *Wilhelm Meister's Apprenticeship* (completed in 1796, twenty years after its inception), was the general education of the hero, Wilhelm Meister; for the general education of individuals was regarded as the highest individual and social good. But the second novel, *Wilhelm Meister's Journeyings* (first published in 1821, but not completed till 1829), represents a radical change of view, inasmuch as the hero now concludes that a specialized education for a vocation or profession constitutes the highest individual and social good. Wilhelm Meister chose to become a medical doctor, that is, a healer of men.

Let me attempt at this point, to summarize Goethe's basic thinking regarding the self and its development by a series of short but related quotations from his works.

In his description of the Pedagogical Province in *Wilhelm Meister's Journeyings*, three, actually four, kinds of reverence are demanded of the students, one of whom is Wilhelm Meister's son Felix:

Reverence for that above us as human animals;

Reverence for that on our own plane or level;

Reverence for that below us.

From these three, the highest reverence develops, namely, the reverence for the self. By learning reverence, says Goethe, man develops, indeed it is his moral obligation to develop, to his highest potential, so that he may regard himself as the best which Nature and God have produced.

It is important to note here how a dynamic development of the individual self is combined with a moral imperative of duty. Nature provides individual human beings with various talents, and these must in turn be developed by self-willed and self-directed education or training.

"We posit talents which are to be developed into skills," Goethe says. "This is the purpose of all education. It is the clear and overt intent of parents and superiors, and the silent, half-conscious aim of the children themselves." [30]

It is the imperative function of education, to "direct capabilities and skills toward their proper goals." [31]

"Only by means of diligence and varied practice does the finest talent unfold unexpectedly into a skill." [32]

"The most insignificant capability or talent, is acquired at birth. There is no such a thing as an indeterminable talent." [33]

Furthermore, "our desires are presentiments of the latent capabilities within us, forerunners of what we shall be in a position to achieve." [34]

Obviously, those men (or women) are fortunate "whose jobs (or professions) correspond fully to their inner vocations, and whose earliest development is consistently complemented by their later training, so that their talents develop in a natural way." [35]

Goethe summarized his conception of fully developed human nature (*Menschlichkeit*—'humanness' or 'humaneness') in his essay on Winckelmann, as follows:

> Man is capable of many things through the purposeful use of various individual resources, and capable of the extra-

ordinary by means of combining several resources. But he achieves the wholly unexpected, the unique, when he co-ordinates all of his resources. . . . When healthy human nature functions as a whole, when a human being feels himself to be part of a world which is great, beautiful, dignified, and worthy, and when the feeling of harmony within himself provides him a pure and unrestrained ecstasy, then the universe, if it could possibly be conscious of having reached its fulfillment, would rejoice and be astounded in viewing the pinnacle of its own being and becoming.[36]

All of this theory regarding the continuous dynamic and purposeful development of the self to the highest possible point and by dint of persistent effort, Goethe applied explicitly to himself. Regarding his own personal development, he said in a letter to Lavater:

> The desire to build as high as possible into the air the pyramid of my own being, whose basis was pre-determined and given to me, outweighs everything else and hardly permits neglect for even a second. I dare not let up, for I am getting along in years. Fate may interrupt the process, and thus my Tower of Babel may remain unarticulated [*dumpf*, a key-word of Goethe] and incomplete. But people should, at least, be able to say that the conception was daring. And if I go on living, I am determined, God willing, that my resources shall reach their maximum potential.[37]

And, in *Wilhelm Meister's Journeyings,* "To develop my individuality, quite as it is, was unconsciously from youth on my desire and purpose." [38]

In summary, Goethe regarded the plastic molding of a personality as being analogous to the creation of a work of art. Indeed, the developed human personality is the most sublime work of art, the creation of which constitutes a moral imperative of God, of Nature, and of Man.

In this regard, Goethe exemplifies an aphorism of Friedrich Schlegel, " Many people are dubbed artists who are actually nature's own works of art."

## IV

The practical application of Goethe's theoretical view of the self and its development to his own personality and self-development is perhaps best illustrated by a cluster of interrelated ideas central to his thinking, writing, and doing. These ideas are usually referred to as the demon (*Der Dämon*), character building (*Bildung*), Polarity (*Polarität*), augmentation or enhancement (*Steigerung*), and renunciation (*Entsagung*).

Although it is possible to define and to document each of these axioms in great detail from Goethe's writings and conversations, it is important to keep in mind that, in Goethe's inimitable fashion, these ideas were conceived and used more as symbols or poetic metaphors than as refined pieces of logical or forensic equipment. Particularly the older Goethe tended more and more to subsume all experience in symbols of this kind.[39] To take just one example: The whole idea of *Bildung*, revolving as it does about the thought that each human individual has in him the seed of a thrust forward and upward in response to which he becomes *gebildet*, i. e., developed, or educated, or cultured, receives its classic expression in poetic terms, in the well-known concluding lines of *Faust*,

> Das Ewig–Weibliche
> Zieht uns hinan!

The Woman—Soul leadeth us
Upward and on!

With this couplet, Goethe was saying, in poetic terms, that the development of self does not end with the death of an individual but continues on and on in the after-life, whatever that may be.

Allow me to digress briefly here on an interesting and important analogy between Goethe and contemporary psychoanalysis. Goethe's propensity for expressing his thoughts about personality structure and development in a symbolic language, created expressly for that purpose, has a neat counterpart in the language of psychoanalytic theory, a fact which is not always understood. (And, by the way, let us not overlook the fact that the word "psychiatry" itself is not documented as having occurred in the English language until 1846, fourteen years after Goethe's death.)

In Greek literature and mythology psychoanalysts found what seemed to them classic realizations and expressions of human relations and life situations basic to their theoretical constructs of human personality. So, for example, Sophocles seems to have said the last word on the primal relationship between offspring and parent in his play *Oedipus, the King,* and so psychoanalysis refers to this relationship as the Oedipal relationship. The relationship between offspring and female parent was felt to be fully expressed in the Greek mythological and literary embroidery of Electra, one of the daughters of Agamemnon, and so the complex of depth—psychological relations and tensions of this kind bear Electra's name. Pathological introversion seems perfectly expressed in the story of Narcissus, who fell in love with his own image reflected from the water into which he was contemplatively gazing. His fascination by and his longing for his own image became so irresistible, that he eventually pined away and became the pining flower which bears his name. And so in the language of psychoanalysis pathological introversion is called narcissism.

The importance of such " primordial images " or archetypes, as they appear in poetry, has, of course, received much attention from Carl Jung and is basic to a good many of his psychological theories. And so it is not surprising, though remarkable, that Sigmund Freud's own writings also frequently refer to the ideas and statements of Goethe.

Considerations of this kind were the basis for Dr. Milton Rosenbaum's observation that the arts have given much and still have much more to give to the scientific study and understanding of personality. It is a well-known fact that not Greek literature but Shakespeare allegedly provided Dr. Frederic Wertham with the keystone clue for solving a New York matricide.[40] And I shall always be charmed by Theodor Reik's writing, if only because of that chapter in *Listening with The Third Ear* to which he gives the title *Eine kleine Nachtmusik* after the music of Wolfgang Amadeus Mozart.[41] Indeed, the title of the book *Listening with the Third Ear* derives from a physiological image adapted by Friedrich Nietzsche to the scientific language of the history of culture.

Though psychoanalysis has borrowed heavily from the arts, particularly for its symbolic vocabulary, it has conversely contributed much to the study and understanding of the arts. There are many examples, but I think particularly of two, close to home: As is generally known, Drs.

Richard and Editha Sterba of Detroit have written an illuminating book about the relations between Beethoven and his nephew,[42] and are currently at work on a psychoanalytically oriented study of Michelangelo Buonarotti. As regards " my Goethe " (to borrow Dr. John Dorsey's image and phrase), the Wayne State University Press will next year publish a monumental two-volume study of Goethe under the title *Goethe: A Psychoanalytic Study* by the eminent New York psychoanalyst, Dr. Kurt Eissler.

V

Central to Goethe's whole idea of the developing self was the concept of *Bildung*, the building of character, the building out of the personality to the fullest and highest degree consonant with the innate talent or talents or potential ability of the individual. It is in this sense that we call both the *Meister* novels and *Faust*, poems or novels of *Bildung*, viz., of personal development.

Closely related to the idea of *Bildung* is that of " the demon " (*Der Dämon*), a concept for which Goethe probably owed something to Socrates. The term was a favorite with Goethe, and efforts have been made to define its meaning in precise terms. Perhaps we can best understand it as referring to a drive or series of drives that characterize every human animal. The demon is that " inborn force and personality " (*Orphic Sayings*) which more than anything else determines the life and self of a man.

To Eckermann, Goethe said (March 2, 1831): " The daemonic is that which cannot be explained by reason or understanding; it lies not in my nature, but I am subject to it." [43]

These gremlin-like drives are, like all drives, completely

irrational. They are also very powerful and, to the personality or thing in which they reside, irresistible:

> But this demonic quality appears at its most fearful when it comes forth predominantly in some human being. . . . These are not always the most excellent persons, either in mind or in talents, and rarely commend themselves by goodness of heart. But an enormous force issues from them, and they exert an incredible power over all creatures, and even over the elements. And who can say how far such an effect will extend? [44]

It has been suggested that some of the more oracular sayings of the older Goethe seem as though an old pagan belief in spirits had been revived in him. The demon was one such.

Each demon has enormous potentials for both good and evil, and each individual has the obligation, as part of his *Bildung,* to direct his demon toward realizing the good.

Not only persons, but things and events also are inhabited by the demon. So, for example, Goethe conceived of water as having a demonic power of attraction, much in the manner of the ancient story of Narcissus. He gave wonderful poetic expression to the idea in the original version of his poem entitled "To the Moon" (*An den Mond*):

> Das du so beweglich kennst,
> Dieses Herz in Brand,
> Haltet ihr wie ein Gespenst
> An den Fluss gebannt.

[You, oh softly caressing and tranquilizing moon, know and understand the agitation of my inflamed heart, and you whisper all this to my sweetheart for me, knowing that my heart is like a spectre transfixed by the river.] [45]

In the same way Goethe conceived of certain personalities, both male and female, as having a demonic power of attraction: Napoleon above all, but also Frederick the Great, Lord Byron, Paganini, and Duke Karl August of Weimar, as well as Cleopatra, Lady Macbeth, and Lucrecia Borgia. Goethe regarded his encounter and acquaintance with Friedrich Schiller, his great contemporary compatriot, as having been a demonic event of the first order of importance in his own personal development.

In short, Goethe conceived of the demon or demons as being potentially friendly or hostile, but in any case human beings could not rid themselves of their demons. The demons are one of those primordial conditions or bases of life with which, despite all lack of reason or understanding, men have to learn to live, particularly since each man's demon determines the cast of his character and personality.

One of the sonnets in the *Orphic Sayings* (*Orphische Urworte,* 1817) bears the title *Daimon* (Demon) and reads:

> Wie an dem Tag, der dich der Welt verliehen,
> Die Sonne stand zum Grusse der Planeten,
> Bist alsobald und fort und fort gediehen
> Nach dem Gesetz, wonach du angetreten.
> So musst du sein, dir kannst du nicht entfliehen,
> So sagten schon Sibyllen, so Propheten;
> Und keine Zeit und keine Macht zerstückelt
> Geprägte Form, die lebend sich entwickelt.

> As on that day which blessed the world with thee,
> The sun stood high to send the planets greeting,

Thou soon didst thrive and prosper constantly,
According to the law that gave thee being.
So must thou be, thyself thou canst not flee,
So Sibyls, Prophets long have been decreeing.
No time, no power ever has dissolved
Fixed types that have as living forms evolved.[46]

## VI

Closely related and complementary to the dynamic and expansive concept of *Bildung* are the twin concepts of polarity (*Polarität*) and enhancement (Walter Kaufmann), or intensification (Karl Viëtor) or augmentation or progressive refinement (*Steigerung*). The origins of these two terms in Goethe's thinking, the referents back of the terms, and the application of the terms illustrate and illuminate, perhaps better than any other single item, Goethe's attitude toward all of life, its ultimate meaning, and the part man plays or should play in it.

The ideas of polarity and enhancement derive directly from Goethe's study of nature, his empirical observation of the working of the physical universe. My scope will not permit any enlargement of Goethe's activities and achievements as a working natural scientist. (There is an extensive and diversified literature on this subject available to anyone interested in pursuing it.[47]) It must suffice to note that Goethe operated as a working scientist in the fields of morphology, comparative anatomy, botany, biology, optics, geology, and meteorology. (His writings on the natural sciences comprise thirteen volumes of the Weimar Edition of his works.) His prime point of departure was the expansive nature philosophy that characterized much of the thinking of his day. Counterparts and corollaries of Goethe's thinking can easily be found both in Immanuel Kant and Friedrich Schelling, as well as others. More interesting perhaps from a contemporary American point of view is the fact that Goethe's dynamic nature philosophy was highly colored and influenced by the nascent study of magnetism and electricity which fascinated his day much as atomic theory fascinates ours.

The intensive study of nature and the natural sciences came to Goethe as a clarifying force and experience around the year 1779, viz., at the age of thirty and during his first stay in Weimar. He was to comment often in later life on the significance of his scientific studies for his own development, both as man and as poet; and in a way so characteristic of him, the language of these comments again lends to the experience a poetic cast and coloration which gives perfect expression to the intensity and uniqueness of the quality of the experience itself.

Thus, in a conversation with D. J. Veit in 1795, Goethe remarked that he was motivated to study natural science by "concupiscence and passion." ("Ich treibe es aus Begierde, aus Leidenschaft.") In a letter to Ness von Esenbeck (April 2, 1828) he alludes to "seductive botany" ("die verführerische Botanik") and to his "limitless inclination to natural science studies" ("meine unbegrenzte Neigung zu den Naturstudien").

From early youth, Goethe conceived of nature as being a unity, but also as being dynamic in character. Basic for him was the question of *Sein und Werden*, of being and of becoming, that is to say, the problem of the permanent and static basis of things by the side of the constant and endless changes in time and in place.

Und was in schwankender Erscheinung schwebt,
Befestiget mit dauernden Gedanken!

And what the eye as wavering, transient knows,
as types in all-enduring thought be molded.
(The Lord God to Mephisto, *Faust*, ll. 348-49)

Goethe's conception of nature is often related to that brand of Ionian thought which the history of philosophy calls hylozoism (literally: " wood-life ") , viz., that matter is animated and that life and matter are an inseparable unity. Nature is a living something which is active in an eternal cycle. Though unified, nature continuously separates into multiple and infinite particularities as a result of its eternal movement, only to have the particularities recombine again and endlessly into new unities. (The similarity to Hegel's dialectic is immediately apparent and more than a coincidence.) All nature continuously builds and destroys, and this endless activity exists only in the present. It knows neither a past nor a future. It just keeps going on forever and ever.

Now, the eternal movement in nature results from the operation of the principles of polarity and enhancement. In agreement with Schelling, Goethe was convinced that movement or activity in nature resulted from the continuous interaction between the opposing or antagonistic forces which are basic to all nature. From the endless operation of the polar principle of attraction and repulsion, a continuous refinement and enhancement of the particular specifics or forms of nature ensue. Permanence and change manage to exist side by side in complementary fashion.

Again, and in a characteristically most Goethian fashion,

what he thought he observed as an operating basic principle in the non-human universe Goethe transferred to the world of human beings, to the intellectual, spiritual, and artistic dimensions of human activity, and particularly to his own self; for the self is also a part of unified nature. He was convinced that his own *Bildung* resulted from the operation of the twin principles of polarity and enhancement, the principles underlying the basic rhythm of all nature, human and non-human. For Goethe, love and hate were a simple but obvious illustration of one of the polar antinomies which motivate human will and action. In our day, psychoanalytic theory has made this antinomy commonplace for explaining and healing the sick self.

I have several times remarked how characteristically Goethe's own language expresses and communicates the unique and "*self*-ish" qualities of his feeling–thinking. And again, the proof of this allegation is perhaps best given by having you listen to some of Goethe's comments about his understanding of polarity and enhancement and of the antinomies which characterize and define nature and living and the self.

From the *Campaign in France* (November, 1792):

> In Kant's scientific writings, I had grasped the idea that attraction and repulsion are essential constituents of matter and that neither can be divorced from the other in the concept of matter. This led me to the recognition of polarity as a basic feature of all creation, a principle permeating and animating the infinite range of phenomena.[48]

From the *Principes de philosophie zoologique* (1832):

> Separating and coordinating are two inseparable acts of life. Perhaps it is better to say that whether we wish it or

not, it is unavoidable for us to proceed from the whole to the parts and from the parts to the whole. And the more vitally these two functions of the mind are conjoined, like breathing in and out, the better it will be for science and its friends.[49]

From *On Theory of Color* (1801):

Close observers of nature, however diverse their points of view, will agree that everything of a phenomenal nature must suggest either an original duality capable of becoming merged in unity, or an original unity capable of becoming a duality. Separating what is united and uniting what is separate is the life of nature. This is the eternal systole and diastole, the eternal *synkrisis* and *diakrisis*, the breathing in and out of the world in which we move and have our being.[50]

From *The Good Women* (1801):

[Seyton:] Our disposition seems to consist of two sides that cannot exist without one another. Light and darkness, good and evil, height and depth, nobility and vulgarity—these and many other pairs of opposites blended in variable proportions seem to be the ingredients of human nature; and when the artist has painted an angel white, light and beautiful, how can I blame him for conceiving the idea of painting a devil black, sullen, and ugly? [51]

From *Elucidation of the Aphoristic Essay on Nature* (1828):

What makes that essay [*Die Natur. Aphoristisch,* 1781-82] fall short of fulfillment is its ignoring of the two great drives of all nature: the concept of polarity and that of enhancement [*Steigerung*], the former belonging to matter in its material aspect while the latter pertains to matter in its spiritual aspect. The former reveals itself in ceaseless attraction and repulsion, the latter in a perpetual surge upward. But inasmuch as matter can never exist as an active principle divorced from spirit and vice versa, so matter has the faculty of dynamically rising to higher levels and the spirit, conversely, asserts matter's prerogative of attraction and repulsion on its part. . . .[52]

From *Wilhelm Meister's Journeyings* (1829):

Thinking and doing, doing and thinking—that is the sum of all wisdom, recognized and practiced from of old, yet not understood by everyone. Like breathing in and out, both should occupy life in a ceaseless alternating flux; like question and answer, neither should occur without the support of the other. The genius of the human understanding whispers this maxim into the ears of every newborn babe. He who abides by it, checking thinking against doing, doing against thinking, cannot go astray, or if he should, he will soon find himself back on the right path.[53]

Finally, and with special reference to Goethe's own awareness of the importance of his language in expressing his scientific and philosophical thought, he wrote:

Regardless of how variegated, complex, and unintelligible this [metaphorical, symbolic] language frequently strikes us, its basic elements remain the same. Nature rocks itself back and forth by quiet balance and counterbalance, and thus there arises a hither and yon, an up and down, a fore and aft which condition all phenomena we encounter in time and in space. We become aware of these movements and modifications in widely differing ways: on occasion, as simple repulsion and attraction, as a flashing and then disappearing light, as movement of the air, as convulsion of the body, as acidification and de-acidification, but always as something binding or separating, and (all of these movements and modifications continue) agitating existence, and advancing some form of life. Because we incline to believe from time to time that that balance and counterbalance, to which we referred, seem to have disproportionate effect, we have also tried to determine and designate that relationship. And everywhere we have observed a more-or-less, an effect and counter-effect, action and passivity, propulsion and retardation, violence and moderation, male and female. Thus there arises a language, a symbolism which one likes to use and apply to comparable phenomena as allegory, as closely related expression, as literally applicable term.[54]

This documentation of the dynamism of Goethe's thinking and feeling would seem to support Santayana's rejection of Goethe as being the great spokesman and representative of expansive, open-ended romanticism, were it not for one other very important corollary of Goethe's thinking and living—the idea of renunciation (*Entsagung*). This facet of Goethe goes unmentioned by Santayana, almost as though he were completely unaware of it. But it is difficult to believe that one so learned as Santayana regarding Goethe was not aware of it, inasmuch as all of the major works of Goethe's old age culminate in an emphasis on the necessity and propriety of renunciation. By renunciation he meant not asceticism or passive resignation, for Goethe always emphasized the positive and the active, even the aggressive. Thus, even renunciation ultimately becomes a pleasure, that is, something affirmative and constructive. Renunciation means simply the affirming acceptance of the realization that taking implies also leaving whatever life has to offer. In other words, human beings as thinking animals need to make choices in a rational and ordered manner. To make choices means to say both *yea* and *nay*, as occasion may suggest or require. Human beings must learn affirmatively to curb as well as to satisfy their human appetites.

These seemingly contradictory and paradoxical thoughts Goethe repeatedly subsumed in aphoristic statements:

In *W. M.'s Journeyings*: " The intelligent person needs only to control himself, in consequence whereof he will be happy." [55]

*In W. M.'s Apprenticeship*: Man " will not be happy, until his unrestricted striving provides its own limitation." [56]

In *Maxims and Reflections*: " Man's whole artfulness consists of giving up his existence, precisely in order to exist." [57]

In a letter to Carl Ernst Schubarth (1820): " One gives life up, in order to be." [58]

In magnificent poetry, Goethe summarized and symbolized the ambivalence of his idea of *Entsagung* (renunciation, moderation, control, discipline) with the oft quoted phrase *Stirb und werde*! (" die, and thus become "), in the concluding stanza of a poem called *Selige Sehnsucht* (*Blissful Yearning*):

> Und so lang' du das nicht hast,
> Dieses: Stirb und werde!
> Bist du nur ein trüber Gast
> Auf der dunklen Erde.
>
> And until with this you're blessed
> " Die, then live all over! "
> You are but a wretched guest
> In this world—a rover.[59]

Goethe learned self-discipline and the need to renounce, beginning when he was about twenty-six or twenty-seven years old, in connection with and as a result of his practical duties and responsibilities at the ducal court of Weimar. One seems to be reading the libretto of a musical comedy set in Graustark when one learns that, in addition to being tutor and privy-counselor to the Duke, Goethe served as prime minister, secretary of the treasury, director of the theater, curator of museums, secretary of the interior, responsible for the maintenance of roads, forests, and mineral resources, secretary of defense, and court poet of Weimar. Add to these duties his enormous correspondence with leading personalities within as well as without Germany, and his heavy social obligations as lion of the court, and the burden of his obligations becomes incredible. To successfully discharge such varied and multiple obligations obviously required a good deal of self-discipline and the necessity to renounce innumerable attractions and enticements. The catalog of Goethe's practical activities in Weimar readily destroys any image one may have had of Goethe as a young Byronesque romantic poet with a laurel wreath on his brow and no more serious thought in his head than the next encounter with his current lady-love.

But even though his experience as an important man of affairs at Weimar helped to teach Goethe self-discipline, one must also remember that discipline and renunciation were a necessary consequence of his life maxim and goal—the harmonious development of his personality. Balance and moderation by the side of imaginative thrust are necessary and natural complements of the personality in precisely the same way that permanence and change, *Sein und Werden,* complement each other in juxtaposition in the macrocosm.

Indeed, the idea of renunciation became a major preoccupation of Goethe, and he dealt with the problem more than any other creative writer of his time.

" The generalist develops into nothing," Goethe wrote in one of his essays. " Limitation (i. e. discipline) is essential to anyone desiring to make something significant of himself." [60]

Goethe bemoaned the dangerous tendency of his (romantic) contemporaries toward fragmentation and the lack of concentration. He was critical of their diffidence in reaching firm decisions and their reluctance toward planned activity, including practical professional activity or involvement. He complains, that it seems " No one has any conception that the individual must resign himself, if he wants to amount to something." [61]

As with all other components of his thinking–feeling, Goethe also conceived of renunciation in polar and ambivalent terms. Every human being, as human being, has to have his share both of happiness and of unhappiness, of fulfillment and of renunciation, of sadness and gladness (to cite the words of Rabbi Leo M. Franklin)—and thus it is that renunciation, too, eventually becomes a pleasure.

It is well to remember that, contrary to a popular and widespread misconception of the nineteenth-century myth of the Olympian Goethe, Goethe also had his share of personal unhappiness. Contemporary commentators, e. g., Emil Ludwig and Barker Fairley, emphasize Goethe's frustrations, his youthful toying with the notion of suicide in the manner of Werther, and later in life, particularly after his return from Italy, his periodic despondency and feelings of hopeless dissatisfaction with his lot.

I remarked earlier that all of the major imaginative works of the older Goethe culminate in the theme of renunciation. I had in mind, particularly, *Die natürliche Tochter* (*The Natural Daughter*), *Pandora,* and *Stella.* The conclusion of *Stella* was recast in the light of the idea of renunciation. The idea appears most clearly developed in discursive language in the concluding part of Goethe's autobiography *Dichtung und Wahrheit* (*Poetry and Truth* or *Fact and Fiction*).

In poetic terms, the idea of renunciation receives its classic expression in *Wilhelm Meister's Journeyings,* which, not at all incidentally, bears the subtitle *Die Entsagenden* (*The Disclaimers* or *The Renouncers*). Indeed, a good case has been made for interpreting the Meister novels and *Faust* as two complementary fragments of the great confession, the term Goethe was fond of applying to the whole body of his writings.[62] Whereas *Faust* is the modern poetic epitome of the Lucifer-like thrust of the human being to attain the infinite, that is, the Promethean or Faustian thrust and arrogant disclaimer of human limitation, the Meister novels recognize the need in human affairs of discipline and control, of moderation and renunciation. The relation between Meister and Faust is, then, a polar and ambivalent one. The modern ultimate answer to life's problem cannot be given in terms of either-or. The answer must come, rather, in the ambivalent terms of both-and. In the modern world man must so discipline himself and so live, that the angels will say of him, as they do of Faust:

> Wer immer strebend sich bemüht,
> Den können wir erlösen.
>
> Whoso with fervent will strives on,
> We angels can deliver.
>
> [*Faust,* ll. 11936-7]

At one and the same time, however, modern man must learn to become a disclaimer or renouncer, as Wilhelm Meister did in deciding to become a healer of men and a physician, that is, a doer.

These two protagonists, Wilhelm Meister and Johann Faustus, thus represent the two souls in a single breast to which Goethe alludes in his lyric drama *Tasso*. The play has two " heroes," one the talented and hypersensitive poet Tasso, the other the practical man-of-affairs Antonio. The fulcrum of the poem-play is the polar and complementary relation between these two mutually exclusive characters. The play is autobiographical, inasmuch as it symbolizes the two souls in the breast of the poet-statesman Goethe and the polarization of the contradictory facets of his self, that is to say, Gothe's renunciation of an either-or choice, and his insistence on bringing the contradictory and opposing elements of his personality into an enhanced, harmonious, positive, and productive balance.

## VII

I should not like to conclude my discussion of Goethe's conception of personality and individuality without some mention, however summary, of Goethe's attitude toward America. His interest in America also reflected and corroborated his conception of individuality. America excited him primarily as a manifestation of a new world aborning which would provide added opportunities for development to the human imagination and will.

Let me remind you that Goethe was only twenty-seven years old at the outbreak of the American War of Revolution. Like most of his young European contemporaries Goethe became enormously interested in the revolt of the colonies and in his *Autobiography* (IV, Book 17) he alludes to the fact that "the names Franklin and Washington (note the order of priority) began to shine and glitter against the political and military heaven."

In June, 1818, Goethe's attention was attracted to a new map of America which appeared in Parker Cleaveland's book, *An Elementary Treatise on Mineralogy and Geology* (Boston, 1816). Goethe's interest in the book ensued from his scientific studies, inasmuch as the book contained a description and a map of American geology. In 1825, Count Bernhard, the second son of Duke Karl August of Weimar, made a trip to the U. S. A. Goethe read the Count's travel diary carefully and with great interest. When the Count returned to Weimar in 1826, Goethe wrote a poem (*Das Segel steigt!*, September 15, 1826) in his honor.[63] In 1827 (February 21), in conversation with Eckermann, Goethe emphasized the necessity of a Panama Canal. Indeed, there are many references and allusions to America in Goethe's works, his journals, and his conversations, and American visitors to the Court of Weimar were always surprised at his minute knowledge of America and of American affairs.[64]

Among Goethe's *Epigrams and Sayings* (*Sprüche*) there is a poem (1827) inscribed *To the United States* (*Den Vereinigten Staaten*) which gives expression to his buoyant hope for the new world.

> Amerika, du hast es besser
> Als unser Kontinent, der alte,
> Hast keine verfallenen Schlösser
> Und keine Basalte.
> Dich stört nicht im Innern
> Zu lebendiger Zeit,

Unnützes Erinnern
Und vergeblicher Streit.

America, thy lot is better
than this old continent's, our own.
No ruined castles thee enfetter,
no lava turned to stone.
Nor useless memory
nor futile strife
perturb thee deeply
in the midst of life.
To present happiness give sway!
And once your children start to write,
may fate be kind and keep away
all tales of robber,
ghost and knight.[65]

## VIII

To me Goethe's personality is that of an infinitely youthful, hopeful, optimistic striver in the spirit of his own Faust. In the firm conviction that mortal men were created in the image of God, he strove throughout his long and productive life to develop that reverence for self by means of which he could realize and achieve the full potential of his talents. It has been said that Goethe's greatest work of art is his own life. That always seemed to me among the highest tributes that could be paid any artist.

To read and study Goethe, to make him one's own is a most rewarding experience. Barker Fairley has given a magnificent summation of this view:

> The basic state of disturbance which prompts highly endowed individuals to moralize or to philosophize or to create

in one of the arts was more than usually acute in Goethe and more than usually persistent. It is here at the pre-philosophical level rather than in philosophy proper that we must look for the center or focus which initiated and interrelated everything (for Goethe). A difficult thought and yet a simple one, like so much of Goethe, who is himself both simple and difficult. It is here too that we must seek the clue to the influence he acquires over his readers. There is no other word that fits, though we do not customarily speak of an author as influencing us. What happens is that the intimate relation in him between living and writing transfers itself to us as an intimate relation between living and reading. This is not the way we read Homer or Shakespeare. The impact of *King Lear* and the twenty-fourth book of *The Iliad* is greater. But if we ask, in conclusion, which of the three has the power to change men from what they were and make them different, the answer must be Goethe, who alone among very great writers puts himself in this direct personal contact with those who yield to him.[66]

V

# The Growth of Self-Insight

*by*

JOHN M. DORSEY

# *The Growth of Self-Insight*

## MAN LIVING CONSCIOUSLY

It seemed not enough to have taken in the whole circle of arts, and the whole compass of nature, to supply his maxims and reflections; all the inward passions and affections of mankind, to furnish his characters; and all the outward forms and images of things for his descriptions; but wanting yet an ampler sphere to expatiate in, he opened a new and boundless walk for his imagination, and created a world for himself in the invention of fable.

*Pope,* Preface to Homer's *Iliad*

As EXPONENTS OF the practicality of *growing* self-insight I selected three great-minded persons, Thomas Jefferson, Ralph Waldo Emerson, and Johann Wolfgang Goethe. Each has now been considered for his comprehensive appreciation of grown human individuality by a devoted biographer, respectively, Professors Bernard Mayo, Wilbert Snow, and Harold A. Basilius. Professor Milton Rosenbaum, an insightful student of human health, developed the theme, "The Whole Individual; A Health View." From the many comprehensive observations of each of these lectures I have selected only several to illustrate my invigorating truth: Living is an adventure in self-helpfulness which, consciously appreciated, adds the zest to living which it withdraws from dying.

Professor Mayo reported that Jefferson realized his individuality needed caring cultivation. Jefferson made it clear that his mind's use of satisfaction lived best and most through the realization of his life's fullest development. He did not separate service to his own private interests from his developing himself as an American and world citizen. He appreciated the centrality of conscious human will (freedom) as one man's civilizing power, " As long as we may think as we will, and speak as we think, the condition of man will proceed in improvement."

It is enlivening to review self-conscious meanings such as Professor Mayo records of his beloved Jefferson: " He was convinced that man himself—by self-insight, self-education, self-discipline—could overcome . . . or at least divert or minimize ' his possibilities as a destroyer.' " " The key to an understanding of Thomas Jefferson—the mainspring of his thought and action—is human integrity." " The Declaration drafted by Jefferson, and approved by Congress on July 4, 1776, . . . gave new meaning to human aspirations when it proclaimed the primacy of individuals, possessing sacred and inviolable rights, and insisted that man was not made for the state but rather that the state was made by and for man."

Professor Mayo remarked Jefferson's " lifelong and incredibly industrious process of self-insight, self-education, and self-discipline." Jefferson did not view mankind as if a few were great and the rest small. He saw all as great, but only a few as aware of this greatness in themselves.

He said, " The people themselves are the only safe depositories of government," and " To render even them safe, their minds must be improved." Surely the only possible human freedom is freedom of mind. Conscious freedom of mind, great-mindedness, is attained by gradual increments of self-discovery. Every bit of this way is beset with resistances to self-discovery. I have a human health axiom which never fails: Whatever seems farthest fetched in my mind is that which needs to be brought closer. Self-consciousness is the specific democratizing force energizing the sense of self-sufficiency, the equalizer.

Professor Snow's Emersonian learning is by heart, not by rote. Observing him naturally delivering himself of Emersonian insights it was easy to conjure up a strong physical resemblance of Professor Snow and the Concord Sage:

> Trust thyself: every heart vibrates to that iron string.
>
> The purpose of life seems to be to acquaint man with himself.
>
> He is not to live to the future as described to him, but to live to the real future by living the real present.
>
> A man should learn to detect and watch that gleam of light which flashes across his mind from within, more than the lustre of the firmament of bards and sages.
>
> Nothing is at last sacred but the integrity of your own mind.
>
> Discontent is the want of self-reliance: it is infirmity of will.
>
> I am divine. Through me God acts; through me, speaks. Would you see God, see me; or see thee, when thou also thinkest as I now think!

Poet Snow reported upon Emerson's realization of education as being self-development. " It is only as man puts off all foreign support and stands alone that I see him to be strong and to prevail. He is weaker by every recruit to his banner." Again "That which each can do best, none but his Maker can teach him." "This is my boast that I have no school follower. I should count it a measure of the impurity of insight, if it did not create independence."

It takes self-consciousness to dispel such stage effects as hero and villain. The clue to a happy full life is to be able to see clearly all that is in that life. The correspondence of self-living with recognition of self-living,—that is self-insight. No change of circumstances can repair a defect of character, said Emerson. "In all my lectures, I have taught one doctrine, namely, the infinitude of the private man." One must atone (at one) when one is at sixes and sevens with himself.

Professor Rosenbaum expertly presented the healthfulness in an individual's respecting his wholeness, stating that health means wholeness. He indicated that by "whole individual" he referred "to the stage of psychological and physiological development of man which allows for a meaningful interplay between the world-outside-and-the-self and that which we are wont to call the self's inner world." He brought clinical experience and research data to bear upon the fact that mental health is the product of a person's way of life. His extensive professional experience had demonstrated that health is engendered when a person works out a harmony of his outer and inner world.

Dr. Rosenbaum went on to speak of a physician's helping himself by the "age-old injunction 'Know Thyself.'" Speaking out for motivation of self-awareness, he said, "In the practice of medicine it would be hoped that such motivation would accrue from a conscious awareness of the importance of self-knowledge in enhancing the efficacy of the physician as a healer of the sick." In spite of all of the formidable internal and external obstacles to this ideal of self-insight, declared Dr. Rosenbaum, "I continue to believe in the possibility of developing better awareness of one's inner self with a view to becoming more mature and more whole."

The central problem of all philosophers and psychologists has always been the same one: How to feel self with whole self-certainty in object as well as in subject. It is of the most practical and immediate life-saving importance for the physician that he live his patient in the kindest and most skillful way possible. How therapeutic Walt Whitman's soul-sight!

> Agonies are one of my changes of garments,
> I do not ask the wounded person how he feels,
> I myself become the wounded person,
> My hurts turn livid upon me as I lean on a cane
> and observe.

John Dewey posed a grave medical problem, "Our language is so permeated with consequences of theories which have divided the body and mind from each other, making separate existential realms out of them, that we lack words to designate the actual existential fact." [1]

Anything and everything that disturbs my sense of being a human whole dispirits me. It is my fullest sense of personal identity which provides me with my highest morale, with the bracing tone and vigorous resistance characteristic of accessible vitality. There are drugs for putting me to sleep and for exciting me in my dream of being awake,—but there is no drug for my waking myself up to myself. Emily Dickinson sang,

No drugs for consciousness can be;
Alternative to die
Is nature's only pharmacy
For being's malady.

It is helpful to observe the center of gravity as well as the center of levity in all humor. Laughter which applies consciously only to the humorous and neglects the serious side of a joke is of the nature of insane laughter. With this introduction, I offer the story of the man who appears at his doctor's office with a lump on the back of his neck large enough to fill out a derby hat. The physician offers to remove the lump but the patient draws back in alarm, crying out, " I don't want that removed. How do I know that I don't do my thinking with it! " Every organ of the body is physiognomic. The wise diagnostician today recognizes that his body is in one way or another disclosing the behavior of his mind and the conduct of his life. The benefit of this insight is Dr. Rosenbaum's.

Professor Basilius presented his mind-conscious Goethe as a life affirmer, as a yea-sayer recognizing the humanistic meaning of self-reverence. Thus, " To develop my individuality, quite as it is, was unconsciously from youth on my desire and purpose." Professor Basilius observed comprehensively:

" There is probably no comparable personality in western history to whom the problem and question of the self was so central as it was to Goethe."

" It has been said that Goethe's greatest work of art is his own life. That always seemed to me among the highest tributes that could be paid any artist."

" Goethe's writings and recorded conversations are replete with observations concerning the self, the importance of development of the self, and the ways in which the development of the self can and must be done."

Pointedly insightful is Professor Basilius's comment, " And it is precisely this concern with the self and its development, this basic concern with the growth of self-insight which made Goethe so contemporary and, if I may say so, so American." Emerson copied in his journal this excerpt from Goethe, " A strong nature feels itself brought into the world for its own development, and not for the approbation of the public."

To attend to my all as selfness is the only way for me to see, or feel, its humanity status. How beautifully Goethe said it,

> And all for me the flowerets grew
> That on each meadow richly flourished.

Professor Basilius called attention to Goethe's appreciation of American liberty, " His interest in America also reflected and corroborated his conception of individuality. America excited him primarily as a manifestation of a new world aborning which would provide added opportunities for development and achievement to the human imagination and will." In America it is only being patriotic to consider oneself a world, rather than a member of a narrow governmental cult. The only safe and sane sovereignty of the individual is his development within himself of an aristocracy of humaneness. Living *is* affirming; dying is the mephistophelian " spirit that denies."

The individual's learning process (the creation of personal meaning), as Professor Basilius indicates, is the central principle involved in the development of the mind and the growth of humaneness. Goethe saw and named his

" inner universe," closely studied it, elaborated upon it in his writings, and enjoyed its salutary action as he lived out his productive life. Said he, only life teaches everyone what he is.

## INSIGHT REVEALS HUMANENESS

> I have never met a scientist who had become cultivated (in the humanistic sense) by virtue of his scientific education or by his subsequent work as a scientist.
>
> *T. N. Whitehead*

Meaning is the unit of the mind itself. With characteristic presence of mind Freud held meaning to be: significance, intention, tendency and position in a course of mental events. All that is mental (mind, the manifold of meaning) exists *an sich,* unrelationally. In *The Meaning of Meaning* C. K. Ogden and I. A. Richards write, " We must suppose that the mind was MEANINGFUL from the very outset," and, " from the psychological point of view, MEANING is context." [2] Meaning is a synonym for being; meaningless is a synonym for non-existent. Insight (seeing every meaning as self-property) is the unit of mental health. Insight is a synonym for consciousness. Conscious, compounded of *con* and *scio* (to know), means knowing within one's self. Self (human) is the all of the person's individuality, and the only place where human being exists. Only by means of my self-insight can I summon the presence of mind to see myself as an end rather than as a means. Indeed, my careful observation reveals every so-called " means " to be an unrecognized end anyhow. All successful efforts at humanization are based upon the realization that each person is his, or her, own end. Real, from *res,* means belonging to the thing *as it is.* Reality, whatever is, is all and only existence. Every human being is born an individual, but is not born with comprehensive insight that his individuality constitutes his all, his entire experience, his whole world. The growth of this kind of insight is the cultivation of his sanity. The unique *itselfness* of all of its activities is what distinguishes individuality.

A note about my use of language is called for. I have observed that popular Language is apt to be misleading on any subject. With Steele I take heed, the first steps in the breach of a person's integrity are more consequential than is recognized. I have tried to choose words which tend to describe the fact that I am writing only of my own individual experience. Therapeutic linguistics respect the one truth: "The subject is one with the object."[3] Thus, if I wish to express the idea that I am traveling "from one place to another," I may use the prefatory words, "I live myself as 'traveling from one place to another.'" Or, if I wish to refer to anything or anyone of my external world, I may introduce such a view by a reference to the fact that *I live* the "whatever" or "whomever" that I have "on my mind." In other words, the *general* truth which provides the *particular* whatever or whomever I "have in mind" is my living of the whole experience. Why I use this vocabulary which features self-reference will become clearer when I discuss the method of awakening the perception of personal selfhood. Nothing is of such benefit to humanity as the discovery of the only place where it is to be found: in human individuality.

Walt Whitman noted the need of man for a vocabulary

which properly observes each one's unique creaturehood: "The new world, the new times, the new peoples, the new vista, need a tongue according—yes, what more, will have such a tongue—will not be satisfied until it is evolved." "Words follow character nativity, independence, individuality."

It gratifies me to be keenly appreciative of everyone whom I have lived as my teacher. To all of this student life (self-discipline) I am obligated for my sustained interest in my planned self-development. In my personal and professional life it pleases me to note the very great extent to which my self-helpfulness is achieved by, so to speak, standing upon the shoulders of my Sigmund Freud. Professor Freud dared to open his mind's eye, *consciousness,* and accept its evidence, *selfness.*

Over one hundred years ago, Emerson said, "We want one miracle by way of evidence: namely that a mind not profound should become profound. The teaching which has that miracle to show will go round the world." The psychoanalytic method is going around the world. The extension of an individual's self-consciousness is his specific way of discovering the profundity of his mind. Self-insight works a wonder by enabling escape from the repression (self-ignoration) always associated with didactic teaching. "Learning has taken place when any part or aspect of the ongoing life process remains with one." [4]

In the observations to follow I do not aim at producing conviction—I am already convinced that each statement is all and only about me, about my way of helping myself. As Thoreau viewed his life, "One world at a time." Only within each one's own life can all mankind meet. I realize full well that everyone else has the ability to help (that is, live) himself in his own peculiar way, and I would also be interested in having an account of that way. I do not aim at securing another's understanding, for I am certain that it is only possible for the given individual to understand, or misunderstand, himself. I cannot understand or misunderstand (my) another; I have (my) him do that.

The observations which I make are not arguments. I do not argue; I declaim. Argument implies that each disputant cannot be talking about the same thing. Each one can talk only about, and to, himself. Judgment and logic are only expedient mental makeshifts. Hail Pascal's bright brevity, " Two extravagances: to exclude Reason, to admit only Reason." The natural flow of mental events (" free association ") *is* most meaningfully reasonable but too rarely *consciously* considered, and therefore hardly ever observed as one's own helpful mental happenings. However, such self-consciousness provides the greatest self-appreciation and the most extensive self-supervision. Seeing my every word *as* mine, as being a growth of myself, is self-sight (self-insight), my conscious purpose. I. A. Richards wrote for his educator, " Learning that is fruitful in such a matter as the development of the most highly organized of man's activities, the control of his thought through language—is better treated as growth from within; and *that* feels, as we make it, like insight." [5]

Not only " can " I augment my fund of self-insight, but also I *must* do so in order to protect my own health and happiness. I am always sole heir of all of the content of each preceding moment of my existence. I exert myself to grow this self-insight (to enlarge my ability to see that my life is all and only about me) for I am afraid not to do so. Ignored selfness is oppressed and rebellious selfness.

Stevenson contended, "Selfishness is calm, a force of nature: You might say the trees are selfish." As I observe with my medical students: I make myself conscious so that I can avoid making myself cancerous, contagious, criminal, contentious, and otherwise crazed.

Thus Whitman described Emerson, "A just man, poised on himself, all loving, all inclosing, and sane and clear as the sun." And Emerson declared, "We are as much informed of a writer's genius by what he selects as by what he originates." Man's supreme mental power, uniquely his own, is his marvelous capacity for self-consciousness. As might be expected, the way in which he uses and cares for this insight-providing "mind's eye" of his decides the degree of his mental health. Aversion to self-consciousness begins in one's earliest mind-forming years as a means of "forgetting" one's painful personal living; then it hardens into a habit. Restriction of the zone of my life which I can call my own and cherish as such (be self-conscious about) accounts for *all* of my mental disorder. The object and contents of the science of mental health may be simply stated: The study and practice of self-consciousness. John Dewey learned, "The discipline that is identical with trained power is also identical with freedom."

My mind has strengthened and healed itself in one way only: by extending its sense of its own self-subsistent identity, the only process by which I have been able to extend my consciousness of my living, growing self. I do not stop living (only) myself, whether I am studying or "visiting." I must live my everyone and everything as vital selfness of my own. The hygienic condition of all method in pedagogy is that it be intentionally heuristic.

As Rousseau put it, for the education of Emile, " Let him not learn science, let him invent it."

All of the experiences which a person lives *which contribute to his proper self-esteem and observed one-being* are so many educational processes strengthening his mind. That only the extreme of one is fully one is a view which fairly expresses my personal, including doctrinal, solipsistic life orientation. All of the growing human being's opportunities to appreciate his self-power, to develop his capacity for *conscious* self-reliance, self-possession and self-appreciation are specific safeguards against mental trouble. Marjorie Brierley has discovered for herself that " every personal attempt to live integratively is a direct, if minute, contribution to the raising of the psychological standard of life for all." [6]

Being an individual, an integer, I can be made up of nothing but my oneness. This statement provides my natural basis of morality. My natural ethical standard, which works, is the product of my increasing my self-awareness to be able to realize that a hurt to my fellow man is a hurt to me, a help to my fellow man is a help to me. By " hurt " I mean only limited self-help. Hume observed that every wise man tries to place his source of happiness in that which he can see depends on himself. The stronger my mind the more it appreciates that life, fully considered, envolves a continuum of difficulties to be made easy. " We need constantly to remind ourselves that both pleasure and pain can be our teacher, and that we may progress and learn life's lessons as much from the evil as from the good." [7]

I find that I can make my tolerance broad or narrow, that I can observe or ignore my own personal experience;

that I can know myself either " intellectually " or as a *living* wonder; that I can think and feel with or without realizing that my life's essence is in my sensing and perceiving; that I can live my life and use my mind with or without appreciating the vital truth that I am living and minding me. Furthermore, I find that I can forget myself or remember to be aware of my own experience; that I can live my life planlessly or guide myself wisely; that I can make myself feel happy or unhappy; that I can make myself sane or insane; that I can " put on my head " and sense *selfsameness* in all of my worldliness or " lose my head " and sense foreignness in all of my " environmental " living. " Only they have come of age who have learned how to educate themselves. Education, like life, works from within outward." [8]

In all of these ways of my living me, it is my self-consciousness which enables me to be present in my own eyes. It completes my sense of my personal identity quite as my self-unconsciousness depletes my appreciation of my humaneness. The sense of humaneness is always a self's sensation of love. Consciousness is immediate life awareness; and, like every other preception, it is discrete from all judgment and reasoning. With consciousness presiding, there is no scale of values,—all is lovingly appreciated alike as selfness.

A scholarly mind is not necessarily one which has lost its sense of personal identity in the " branches of knowledge." A way of life can hardly be reduced to a science of specific subject matter other than that of the life under consideration. A stinging truth of most practical significance for me, a medical educator, is that I seemingly " humanize " or " dehumanize " my science, depending upon whether or not I clearly recognize all of it as mine, and thereby esteem it as my mental property. *My " dehumanization " is always the product of my mental dissociation.* This mental " dissociation " separates all of my life which I can acknowledge as mine (and hence must sense and observe its humanity) from the rest of my life which I disown as mine (and thereby cannot heed its humanity). To escape thus dissociating my mind I must develop new sensibility to recognize *its* vivid identity in every " phenomenon " and " postulate." Human unity is given; only the ability to appreciate it can be " attained." The same life animates ego and alter.

My humanization is always the product of my consciously sensing my own human identity in my present living, of my renouncing all intersubjectivity as being illusion. Such ordering (conscious compassing) of my mind constitutes my mental health and strength. My troubled mind (" mental disorder ") is a helpful attempt to compensate for, and recover from, a " loss of mind " (which apparent " loss " is really an inhibition of keen appreciation and self-satisfying use of my mental power). Invariably my " dehumanization " is incurred by a process of self-forgetting, of the same nature (naïve realism) as that which I practice by vaguely " forgetting myself " in my work instead of clearly finding myself in it.

During the dawn of modern science the pioneer worker foresaw scientific work as surely promising every man full appreciation of the meaning of his humanity. He did not take into his calculations the possibility that the scientist might be " reliably verifying " views contributing to his own annihilation. He spared himself unhappy predictions both of crude and refined scientific materialism of the last two centuries,—every bit of it an expression of an individual mind unconscious of the extent of its humanistic range. Sir Russell Brain recorded, "If the expanding universe of knowledge is not to carry all the specialists into ever-lasting isolation from each other, and the rest of the world, some attempt must be made here and there to achieve a comprehensive view." [9]

I observe that it is possible for me to seem to get lost ("dehumanize" myself) in my scientific terminological maze, in my general literature, and even in my grammar itself. It is just, and only, by such systematic "losing my presence of mind" that I may *seem* to emasculate my scientific living. However, it is obviously impossible for me to dehumanize, depersonalize, or otherwise denature myself by any kind of my living. All reliance is self-reliance but it is only possible for consciously self-possessed man to glory in that truth. William J. Norton illustrated the sense of self-possession of his Indian guide during a trek in a Canadian wilderness. Unable to find camp, the guide calmly observed, "Indian not lost, camp lost."

Although all human life is only autobiological, and although practice of that new awareness is the purest devotion to human health and happiness,—nevertheless every person from his earliest years on finds it necessary to limit his practice of "calling his world his own." It is only the rare educator who sees his education as a process of homogeneous growth in self-appreciation (rather than as a process of heterogeneous acquisition of rote knowledge). May every educator grow to appreciate (his) Max Stirner's thrill: "My truth is the truth."

My most fundamental source of the life-satisfaction which makes my existence well worth living is *my willing-*

*ness to activate my self-awareness so that I can observe my augmenting vivacity as my own world maker.* Except for my creating it, my world is underived. Towards the man who can extend his self-awareness further than I can I am in the position of pupil. It is hell on earth to be born a god and to live and die with a shrinking and sinking estimate of my adorable self.

During my professional living I found that a specific kind of unvivified conduct of mine, aptly described as living myself unwittingly, left me feeling dangerously self-displeased,—" tired of living," " fed up on life," " a living failure," " empty headed." Only by my consciousness do I attach due importance to me. By viewing myself clearly as needing to help myself I became personally (not " impersonally ") interested in psychotherapy. I discovered it to be my activation of my healthful learning process: growing my self-knowledge with full self-credit and self-satisfaction.

Thus I came to define both healthful education and psychotherapy as: free devotion to extending self-awareness. It is the specific remedy for the learner who has lived his formal or informal education as if he were " working his head off " rather than " working his head on " by means of his study. Scientific completeness is the outgrowth of *conscious* mental integrity. As a man thinketh in his heart, so is he. However, my awakening to the nature of my mind is not the creating of that nature. It was formerly feared that consciousness emphasized undesirable meanings. " It needed much patient and lengthy demonstration to convince the public that this was not the case; that, on the contrary, unconscious tendencies were deprived of most of their power when an outlet into conscious thought was opened up for them." [10]

The scientist's traditional need of unity is a reflection of the necessity he lives under constantly, his own oneness. The philosopher's need of the universal is a reflection of his own all-embracing wholeness. The saint's need of monotheism is a natural expression of his inviolable human integrity. *Individual life* is the only real, hence practical and solid, interest of everyone's personification: "Humanity." Of necessity I am a "one-man" man, that is, a one-world man.

Only education recognized as the learner's self-activity (life process) is compatible with perfect freedom. Schiller put it thus, "All the arts of pleasure grow when suckled by freedom." My scientific zeal for "objectivity" is understandable against the historic necessity for liberation of scientific work from the superstitions of demonic possession. In ridding my scientific living of "demons," however, it is essential that I be able to see that I cannot rid it of myself. Any attempt to do so must be based upon my deceiving myself (that it is possible and desirable). Mature insight is always manifest as power of inmost self.

Said Protagoras, "Man is the measure of all things." More than that, man *is* all things to himself,—otherwise the condition obtains which Emerson described, things are in the saddle and ride mankind. My education, which reveals to me the vision of a single knowledge, self-knowledge, prevents mental trouble.

## LANGUAGE OF INSIGHT

> The wise man will esteem above everything and will cultivate those sciences which further the perfection of his soul.
>
> *Plato*

" How many grammarians still regard their science as holding the keys of knowledge? "[11] Painstakingly self-oriented writing is seldom, if ever, acceptable as being scientifically oriented. Even the extreme purist in art tends to repudiate the personal element in his aesthetic feeling. For the majority of readers (hence editors) the sanity-preserving reality of " the first person singular " is acceptable only in plainly acknowledged autobiography and in poetry. The anonymous impersonal pronoun, " one," and the anonymous plural pronoun, " we," are preferred by the circulation editor. Shakespeare used twenty-five thousand words in his plays, every one of them basically a symbol of that precious plenitude, Shakespeare. It may be difficult to find personal meaning in " the nomenclatures of science," but that is all that there is to them. I. A. Richards wrote with wisdom, " Thoughts about language ought to be the most widely stimulating of all mental exercise."[12]

A rewarding (self) study offers in investigating (1) the child's growth of his " received " parts of speech and (2) the mental process by which speech forms now taken for granted were first invented. Certainly the need exists for every tongue to develop itself for mental health purposes. The true direction of that healing process seems straight towards (1) the exposure of the authoritarianism concealed in a " received " vocabulary and (2) the discovery of appreciation of human individuality derivable from valuing words for their use in the development of the language (science) of self. I find it necessary to change my speech habits to keep pace with my growing self-insight. " Learning speech," to me means creating clear, strong and appreciated wording of my mind power. Walter B. Pitkin claims, "As language is to thinking, so is learning to living." [13]

Sir Thomas Browne introduced the noun "hallucination" to designate a meaning of his own mind; Robert Boyle coined the adjective "pathological" to express a conception of his own making; Carlyle invented the substantives "self-help" and "environment" to distinctify certain of his own mental modifications; Jeremy Bentham first employed the linguistic expression "dynamic" in order to provide himself with a word-picture of his own mental events. Destutt de Tracy created his word "ideology" to distinguish his investigation of his thought, itself. Gottfried Reinhold Treviranus (1776-1837), inventor of the word "biology," intended it as the mental concept which it is. (The creation of this term is also attributed to Lamarck, 1744-1829.)

As Simeon Potter sagely submitted, "Language, after all, is more psychological than logical." In 1840, William Whewell apologized for coining the word "scientist." Definition of a word is always misleading since it implies that one word can be explained by other words. The truth is that every word has its own unique meaning and alone can attest that meaning. The meaning of education as "a specific kind of discipline in self-help favoring healthful living," is highly practical. As I. A. Richards declared, "every mind, however young, realizes when it is awake—that it must be its own keeper." [14]

Not all of the literature of natural science supports Samuel Johnson's assertion, "No man ever read a book of science from pure inclination." Every scientist who enjoys a strong well mind conducts his scientific work feelingly and sees what Thoreau's observation means,

"Nature must be viewed humanly to be viewed at all." Every scientific report is human literature, even if it is not always evident as such. The scientific classics are sensational literature. Everyone's panorama of science is his own "human" psychological production. Scientific writing based upon real observation can only be autobiographical, a record of exploration in the realm of its author's (human) mind.

"The Science of Language expresses man to himself," wrote Michel Bréal, introducing his new science, which he called "Semantics." The English vocabulary is the richest of all. Word-power is always a form of *individual* manpower. Sir Richard Paget pointed out, "Words bear much the same relation to thought that numerals bear to our ideas of quantity." [15] It is sanely practical to keep fresh in mind the historical truth that every word is first and last a mental (human) invention, a poetic phantasy anterior to being used as a scientific term. The nameless poets, word-makers who constructed their own verbal contents and forms, in every instance accomplished this achievement as a mental (human) feat. "Let us marvel anew at the wisdom of that strange, dynamic phrase, 'In the beginning was the word. . . .'" [16]

Everyone grows his vocabulary as if it were a *received* language, unaware that it most inadequately represents respect for his individuality. Before he realizes it he is already using his words to imply that he is able to be "out of his mind." Korzybski dared to say that "we have not, as yet, entirely emerged from a very primitive semantic stage of development, in spite of our technical achievements." [17] The sane use of language transcends its delusional exploitation as a kind of mysterious "communication between " one individual (all) and another individual (all) to become an accurate language of selfhood, a practical means for greater use and appreciation of one's own human life itself. The alternative to this usage is to take words for knowledge, mind-obscuration. Smith Ely Jelliffe scored this point: " To say the facts are incomprehensible is a rationalization of individual ignorance."

Plutarch wrote, " Speech is like cloth of Arras opened and put abroad, whereby the imagery doth appear in figure; whereas in thoughts they lie but as in packs." *My every word has only personal meaning.* All of its interestingness is provided by me. The enormous practical importance of this distinction cannot be appreciated too much. Only from this mine of self can I quarry my power of insight.

The synoptical view of learning to follow is not intended as any kind of " communication," even of dictionary words, there being no such possibility (in its author's opinion). What then is its purpose? *I* am vitally concerned that *my* reader grow as his own *acknowledged* creation, whatever he reads, or otherwise perceives and senses. Although I cannot help my reader, I can be far more helpful than that: *I can grow my reader able to help himself and able to derive the life-sustaining satisfaction inherent in that appreciation of his own power.* A gain to *my* reader is necessarily a gain to me.

It is of first importance to be able to see what *is* important. Of critical consequence for every educator's research is each of the following questions:

What happens to the mind when it learns?

What is the ideally educated mind?

Is learning a soul-ful experience, an activity of the very

essence of me, an exercise of the vital principle? Or is learning a conquest of my life's power by some " external " force? Or, is it both? The professional philosopher, educator and psychologist have been approximating some unanimity in the definition of just what happens in a mind when it learns. Thus, it seems self-evident that the generic function of the cognitive (learning) process is that of providing knowledge about the learner's own life. However, sensory experience, which is the mental function at the very root of the educative process, is sometimes allocated to a non-human (" impersonal," " external," " physical ") world. By this kind of separation and definition sensation, and even perception, tend to become unrecognized humanity, while conception (including " memory ") and imagination (including " thinking ") may become the only fully accepted *human* elements of the mental activity called " learning."

Traditionally, the psychologist reasons sensation and perception to occupy a borderland which somehow bridges over mental and non-mental powers,—the borderland of " objectivism " and " subjectivism." Thus the vocabulary of the psychologist has tended to lose its force and applicability *as even intending to be* purely psychological. Psychological pedantry is the warning sign, if a psychologist psychologizes as if he could be out of his mind.

" Educational psychology " is a title given to the educator's and psychologist's efforts to see, and thus activate consciously, the humaneness constituting the learning process. However, again the educational psychologist loses track of his goal (consciousness of the humaneness in human learning) if he posits an " external " environment " in which " the biological organism somehow grows itself, instead of positing the human being as growing his environment where he grows all that is his, in his own human being.

On account of vocabulary contaminations, scientific educational and psychological works are replete with literary "bulls" which, without appearing to do so, "change the subject" completely. To illustrate:

> The human biological organism develops in a social medium.
>
> The child's biological potential develops in a specific environment.
>
> External factors influence the development of human personality.
>
> The child learns in school situations.
>
> Society has a role in the educative process.
>
> Whatever impinges on personality affects learning.
>
> Relationships provide tools for learning.
>
> Language enables communication.

## GROWING SELF-INSIGHT AND THE LEARNING PROCESS

> In this country we emphasize both liberal and practical education. But too often it is liberal education for one, and a practical education for another. What we desperately need is an integrated, liberal, practical education for the same person.
>
> *Dwight D. Eisenhower*

My consciousness is the greatest faculty of sentience of my vitality. Its presence ratifies my conviction of my personal identity; its absence nullifies my appreciation of my individuality. All of my reality is grounded in my own being, so that my reality test consists of self-evidence, of a sense of recognition. The absence of my me-feeling, or I-feeling, is certain evidence of self-ignoration (repression). I find my sole authority in my own mind.

Self-knowledge is not at all the same as conscious self-knowledge. Mental integration is not at all the same as conscious mental integration. Every mind is integrated, is a single whole mind, so that minds do not differ in the degree of their integration. Every mind does have its characteristic degree of *conscious* integration, however. That is, every mind is unique in the extent to which its possessor is *aware* of its integration. This wide-awake mindfulness, this *realizing* that all of one's mind is altogether in one piece and place in one's own life, is the specific insightfulness which constitutes the strong healthful mind. *Perfection reveals itself everywhere to insight; it appears to be wanting otherwise.*

Certain questions naturally arise. What kind of educational system cultivates this kind of human excellence? Will such an educational system develop a mind of greatest human virtue? Will its process of learning discipline the learner to be able to observe and *heed* that he is all that he lives and learns about? Will its cognitive process form the best character while the learner is drilling himself in extending his *acknowledged* self-knowledge?

To the first question the answer is, The human system is the only educational system, and the growth of individual human being is the only possible learning process. The *consciously* integrated mind's learning process *is* the growth of self-insight. To the other questions the answer is, Yes. There is no force of human character more natural or noble than that which purposefully steers its possessor to live his world with loving peace through consciously living himself with full appreciation. *Peace is found and bound by the life-preserving sense of personal identity.* I naturally live all that I can see of myself peacefully. Self-awareness enables self-control; self-control dispels illusions and delusions of alien control. Unmanifest egoism is soul-slight, not soul-sight. Shakespeare finely observed the mind unifying power of will:

> If thy soul check thee that I come so near,
> Swear to thy blind soul that I was thy 'Will,'
> And will, thy soul knows, is admitted there;
> Thus far for love my love-suit, sweet, fulfil.

Evident self-knowledge is spiritual as well as technical. The *Kena-Upanishad* recorded, "If in this world a person knows (the Self), then the true end is gained; if a person in this world does not know (the Self) then there will be a great calamity." Man is all that he knows and he must suffer (warn himself) if he uses his knowledge to hide behind. To describe fully is to extol.

Human being is always excellent. A baby, or child, is a complete and perfect human being. Even the word "growing" can be misconstrued to mean "not whole." Every moment of human life *excels.* Amazing material achievements, increasing numbers of ideas, enlarging self-scopes,—all such apparent "changes for the better" tempt one to "look down his nose" upon his past performance and thereby indulge his feeling of self-disesteem as if it refers to his past life. "Health is natural to man, an original outgrowth of his human constitution. This view of the power of self-affirmation, when clear, must essentially reveal all health education as an unfolding of latent and quiescent power within each individual." [18]

When Comte laid the foundation of sociology and implied a science of society to be possible (so that right social conduct could be definitely made law) the question soon arose, What about *individual* man's viewpoint? The sociologist needs the dogma of human progress, and whatever is human occurs only in a given individual human being. *Appraisements of "good," "better," "best," "bad," and "worst" are products of individual man's reasoning,—not of his seeing (insight).*

My idea "human progress" refers only to continuous development of individual man's conscious humaneness. *All that might be properly defined as "progress" is provided only by the going on of my life process, itself.* The "civilization" movement occurs only in the given individual and is the product only of the extension of his self-consciousness. The evolutionary methods of psychozoic man may be directed by him consciously only insofar as he is conscious. And just insofar as he is conscious, man renounces the self-punishment implicit in "lording it over" his past performances. He sees that his present excellence is also a manifest sign of all of his prior excelling.

My one safe and sane aristocracy is my aristocracy of humaneness. Whatever is cannot be improved upon under existing conditions but offers itself as workable reality. The dead past and unborn future are tempting distractions from the lusty and ever insistent present. Terms such as "advancement," "betterment," "improvement," introduce not only the odious but also the impossible: "comparison." Each such term appears to rob Peter to pay Paul.

Comparison introduces illusional "duality," "betweenness," "externality." Quite as J. B. Bury sagely observed, "Progress involves a judgment of value, which is not involved in the conception of history as a genetic process. It is also an idea distinct from evolution."

"Amelioration," like "degeneration," is a term useful to the pained observer who is unaware that he is both subject and object of his painful predicament. During any moment of my life my most useful self-orientation is my acknowledgment that my present living is perfect in every way, that all of my world is exactly as it ought to be, that my living necessitates my being exactly the way I am pending my developing my ability to make myself be exactly otherwise. Shakespeare affirmed, "There is nothing either good or bad, but thinking makes it so." Cultivation of the ability to see all of one's living as perfect, the "divine look," is the only escape from the predicament of value judgment with all of its phantom problems.

Facing the fact that my life is functioning perfectly, even though I may be unhappy, is a confrontation I must fear if it places all of the responsibility for my happiness and unhappiness directly upon myself when I have not developed the self-reliance for coping with such responsibility. By denying the truth of my present perfection and displacing the whole meaning of "perfect" upon my future living I can avoid the hard work of diligent self-help but yet comfort myself with a "doctrine" of perfectibility, of doing something to help myself later on.

I help myself by discovering that I find it useful to indulge ideas of a future "getting better," "improvement," "amelioration," "advancement," "progress," and even "growth" itself, as disguised self-accusations implying unworthiness of my wonderful present living. My devotion to thinking about my " future betterment " is maintained at the cost of devotion to seeing my true *present* worth and, hence, " making the best " of it. " Making the best " of any of my living means seeing that it *is* best—*that* is turning it to health account, by seeing how I help myself with it. It is helpful for me to be able to have every kind of viewpoint comfortably (viz., " I am no good," " I will be better," and so on.) Any self-view which I can see as my own *helpful* creation cannot function as " the tail wagging the dog."

Every kind of learning is obviously traceable only to the learner's personal act of living his self-experience. Hence, *as a matter of self-defense,* everyone evidently tends naturally to uphold the helpfulness of his own particular experience. Thus, " I never got a licking except when I needed it." The study of my learning process therefore is a study of my life's mental process (psychobiognosis). Thomas Davidson defined human education at its best: conscious evolution.

My *complete* act of learning includes:

(1) *my* production of my novel personal experience,
(2) my certain recognition that *I* have created this new self-knowledge,
(3) my duly crediting myself with the fact that my *living it* constitutes my total learning performance.
(4) my appreciating that my test of the degree of my learning is my ability to use what I learn when its use would be opportune.

I am always one (with nothing left over). The only

accurate one is extreme one. However, I can *see* that I am all and only one if and when I am living myself with love. My I-feeling is always increased, never diminished, by my love. Learning by extending my awareness of my life's content, is peaceful living; it is my way of utilizing my personal experience for my welfare, whether or not it is "a prerogative of Life, admitting of no inorganic analogy." [19]

Incomplete learning is humane also but it is not recognizable as all and only a human process. It is well to notice (over and over) that "dehumanization" is always an appearance only, traceable merely to lack of awareness of the ever-present human element. Again, the life-saving significance of self-awareness is seldom given its due. I can rescue my life from the living death associated with self-ignoration only by duly crediting myself with my all-embracing interestingness. "To be or not to be" applies to self-consciousness.

*Real* (sane) education is the learner's consciously attending to his new self-growth until it no longer excites the strangeness of the new, until it is lived with his feeling of identity (sense of selfsameness) in the living of it. Two self-evident truths are needed to free everyone's education from its traditional pretenses of being, and claiming the right to be, capable of violating the inviolable integrity of human individuality:

(1) that each teacher must live (grow) as elements of himself everything which he means by "his pupil,"
(2) that every pupil must live (grow) as elements of himself everything which he means by "his teacher."

The educator, teacher or pupil, is an absolutely free and complete totality. He is an all. What is there left over either to add to, or subtract from, an all? Every particle of man's so-called "relatedness," or "relationship," consists only of his living of it. He cannot know, or be known by, another. Individuality cannot be relational. Einstein eternalized that truth in his relativity hypothesis. His seeing his time-space meanings as being manifestations of his own mind, quite as his beloved Spinoza did, supported his fourth-dimensional views.

*My* learning orientation (that my education is my self-made product) is absolutely essential for my mental health development. Mind consciousness (self-vision) is the foundation and only source of recognized human nature. With this kind of knowingness I escape the trap of self-forgetfulness which ushers in mental trouble. Personal intuition is insightful; "external authority" is insightless. As Ernest Carroll Moore recorded, "Education is the process by which each individual out of his own awareness builds his world." [20]

Only profound ignorance is to be found in the illusion that anyone can in any degree understand, or be understood by, another. Shakespeare's genius laid that ghost (Hamlet to Guildenstern):

> Why, look you now, how unworthy a thing you make of me! You would play upon me, you would seem to know my stops, you would pluck out the heart of my mystery. You would sound me from my lowest note to the top of my compass . . . call me what instrument you will, though you can fret me, you cannot play upon me.

However, may I not pretend to find out something about

"someone else," as a compensation for my very skimpy acknowledgment of my self-extent? I may try, but as Alfred North Whitehead put it, I "cannot divide the seamless coat of learning." Does the tenacity of my delusion that I can know (or be known by) "another," indicate my displaced need for greater *self*-understanding? Have I been afraid to feel "left all to myself" ever since I began overlooking my self-sufficiency by underestimating my greatness through consistently disowning powers of my own life under a false name of Not-I? Apparently just that, for the sake of keeping the peace in my living of (my) authorities.

I define health-making education as: *learning which features the learner's life as willfully creating his self-knowledge.* However, this right (for me) view became clear only as I cleared up my addiction to accepting illusional "companionship" at the expense of rejecting real *aloneness* (all one-ness). I can keep company with myself only. My early fear of being "alone" made me pretend blindly to myself that I was not alone (all one). Fearful superstition, which I discovered was fear of my own rejected authority, blocked my appreciating and consciously exercising my most basic mind-quickening truth: my individuality's allness. I inherit my past moments of self-consciousness as a precious endowment in every fresh moment of my life. Said Thoreau, "I know of no more encouraging fact than the unquestionable ability of man to elevate his life by conscious endeavor."

The mental energy spared for sane living would be sufficient to restore sanity to every educator, if teacher and pupil alike were able to renounce the stultifying superstition of "communication" ("imparting" knowledge and ignorance), and thereby live non-dualistic sanative appreciation for the power of each one to develop his own educational prowess. Over and over I may well repeat: Wholesome use of my language is only for the purpose of distinctifying my own living. I must evolve from my mind whatever I discover about my own world. This mind-strengthening truth can pass unnoticed. *Taking notice* about it is painstaking, painsworthy education to mental health and strength. I need to make the most of my humanity in order to be able to employ it in any educational (including medical) living. This specific appreciation of my life's creative value and synthesizing power is needed for the uninhibited unification of my healthful sense of self-esteem. A. N. Whitehead records, ". . . nature gets credit which should in truth be reserved for ourselves: the rose for its scent: the nightingale for his song: and the sun for its radiance. The poets are entirely mistaken. They should address their lyrics to themselves, and should turn them into odes of self-congratulation on the excellence of the human mind." [21]

It is a mind-disordering view of the educative process which describes it as: the conscious working of the will of the teacher upon the will of the pupil. Such an illusion depends upon its creator's insistence that language functions as if it could be an instrument for " communication." The scientific fact is that education cannot be in any sense: the influencing of one man by another; a reciprocal action " between " human beings; a leading of a follower or a following of a leader; or even the teacher's helping the pupil to help himself. Note Goethe's account of his creation of his " opposite " sex: " My idea of women is not abstracted from the phenomena of actual life, but has been born within me, God knows how. The female characters which I have drawn have therefore all turned out well; they are all better than could be found in reality."

The insightful one's (conscious self-) knowledge consists of truth which he can see and record about himself but admittedly cannot prove to his fellow man. The insightless one's (unconscious self-) knowledge consists of truth which he cannot see (in his own living) but proclaims can be proved to his fellow man. Human individuality counts in education only to the extent that the educator (teacher or pupil) *sees* his humanity in it.

That educational work may persistently offer the false appearance of duality or plurality, of "something going on *between* individuals," is the most (helpfully) distressing bane of its existence. Signs and symptoms of health trials (banes of illness) are always helpful signals. Every pain is a growing pain. This insight constitutes the true therapeutic orientation. "If error is corrected whenever it is recognized as such, the path of error is the path of truth." [22]

All punishment is self-punishment, and avoidance of conscious self-punishment is the specific motivation for self-ignoration. Making a part of myself unconscious to avoid losing consciousness for other parts of myself,—that is a benefit. As ingenious John Cottam noticed of himself, I am punished *by* my transgression and never "for" it. I regard self-punishment as the only accounting for mental oppression ("illness"). Living is awfully wonderful,—suddenly satisfying, suddenly unbearable. As the animal who gnaws off a limb to escape a trap I too can find it helpful to withhold awareness from parts of myself in order that other parts may function freely. In the interest of my own self-control, I must deny my sense of personal identity to my overwhelming life-experience pending my willingness to see it as my own. Wordsworth thoughtfully wrote of self-rejection,

> Who feels contempt for any living thing
> Has faculties which he has never used,
> And thought with him is in its infancy.

I distinguish one " hard fact " from another in the orbit of my life only by the uniquely distinct way in which I live each. However, the only being or reality of any of my knowledge, including its creation, is made up of individuations of my individuality. Very firmly established and traditionally honored are the fiercely defended illusions and delusions which oppose this extreme and exact self-awareness. There is no existence possible for any existent which is not found in *its* being. However, ignoration of my individuality as a unal entity alone accounts for all of my inhumanity in the living of my fellow man. The womb is not the grave of the individual. Full appreciation of the *unicity* of my human being accounts for all of my pleasure in humanely loving my fellow man. Quite as William Law recorded: " You can know nothing of God, of nature, of heaven, or hell, or yourself, but so far as all these things are self-evident in you." An air of omniscience may be becoming to man.

I live comfortably my reader's willful resistance to extending his self-insight,—recognizing such willfulness as a precious undeniable sign of his wonderful individuality. I must depend upon my own sense of equilibrium for maintaining my balance in my walk of life. As well try to walk a tight-rope by using " somebody else's " coordination and poise as depend upon " another's " pleasure and displeasure for the conduct of my life.

It cannot be lived consciously too often: The greatness and power of my human being are disregarded only at the cost of great restriction of my health and happiness. The greater the value the greater the expense involved in any disrespect for the value. Spirituality is the mind's activity which carries the meanings of divinity. Such precious power is repressed (not prized as selfness) as a rule. Discovering one's own divinity (recovering appreciation of it) provides life's most meaningful experience. How direct Whitman's vista, " I should say, indeed, that only in the perfect uncontamination and solitariness of individuality may the spirituality of religion positively come forth at all."

It does appear that every human being is born with *the* most precious feeling, and that soon he does not know what to do with it: his healthy feeling of adoration, of worship. At first it is his natural inalienable expression of his joy of living, of his glorying in his divine life's peace and plenty. Thus, it is obviously applicable to his wonderful life before he sustains many seemingly unholy blows to his sense of self-esteem. All too soon, however, he finds that adoration, the ultimate in life-affirmation, appears to be inapplicable to his uncertain and often exasperating existence. His sense of his own godhood becomes a source of embarrassment, a distressing reminder of his own inability to feel equal to his own life's developments (creations). He solves this problem, of the manifest incongruity of his painful self-observation and his due self-esteem, by allocating his feeling of worship to power sources in his own being which he cannot identify as his own creations and which, therefore, he cannot claim that he controls: *his* mother, *his* nurse, *his* parent. As each of these sources of full life appreciation proves uncertain and exasperating in turn, he disposes of his feeling of his own deity elsewhere in his life, in his god that he cannot identify as his own creation and that, therefore, he cannot feel that he controls. George Bernard Shaw divined, to be in hell is to drift; to be in heaven is to steer.

Only his continuously accurate self-estimate, as entirely divine being, makes accessible to man the abundance of his plenitude and its associated reverence for life. Degrees of self-depreciation are always accompanied by (recognized or unrecognized) signs of ignored divineness, namely, corresponding degrees of obstructed self-functioning and associated limitations of happiness. His adversity, accurately conceived, can only introduce a man to his power. Every great awakening of a person is to new perception of his authority. And acknowledged authority is the only basis for acknowledged responsiblity.

Cicero pointed out that all things are rightly said to belong to the wise man for he alone knows how to use them. Socrates' mental strength was not the product of his general knowledge but of his understanding of the ways of his mind. Urgently needed is research on the nature of the educative process. In 1921, James Harvey Robinson noted that " what we need is education, but something so different from what now passes as such that it needs a new name." And in the 1948 Report of the Commission on Liberal Education of the Association of American Colleges appears: " Young people take inordinate interests in what they think is practical study, failing to realize that self-knowledge, which is indispensable to the most practical judgments, is the highest practicality. In a period of technological prodigies and of economic complexity, the crucial problem of education is to sustain and develop the individual."

Candid Robert Maynard Hutchins observed, " I had mildly suggested that metaphysics might unify the modern university. I knew it was a long word, but I thought my audience of learned reviewers would know what it meant. I was somewhat surprised to find that to them metaphysics was a series of balloons, floating far above the surface of the earth, which could be pulled down by vicious or weak-minded people when they wanted to win an argument." [23]

Humanity-conscious Clarence B. Hilberry noted, " The teacher is in a wonderful position for living generously the meaning of ' wholeness of vision,' which is the creative gift of seeing knowledge, not in pieces, but whole."

## EDUCATION IS BIOLOGICAL

> Who can comprehend his own will, or his personality —that is, his I-ship—or his mind—that is, his person, or his own life?
>
> *Samuel T. Coleridge*

My education is my disciplined learning of my mind to develop and use my powers for myself,—a tried and true guide of my living. The untenable view of education as some mysterious kind of justifiable violation of inviolable individuality, is the most self-insightless of all of my educational perspectives. Another self-insightless one is this invalid but time-honored distinction: Individual growth of the embryo and fetus is somehow more strictly self-development than is individual experience following birth. The biological truth is that every individual originates his education quite as autonomously as he does his hand or foot. Every person's growth of self-knowledge is as innate as is his native growth of any of his other instinct life; it is a natural self-development, an independent original biogenesis, a creation of an extension of his own selfhood, a burgeoning forth of his own internal might. Helpful insights may be derived from regarding the individual's growth *in utero* as a self-activity of the nature of education, a personal education characterized by dearth of personal consciousness. Learning about my world which is not the development of my self-insight, *is* the development of my self-ignoration. "The method of teaching should always be vitalized by the fiery conviction that the pupil is learning to *live,* not going through some sort of rote performance." [24]

Postnatal education, usually called "infant development," consists of quick cramming of life's hardest lessons. A growing baby must learn rapidly to use and enjoy the power of each of his sensory and motor organs. The powerful creation of each of these organs is known as "sensation" and "motion." All of this wonderful biogenesis is describable as "the learning process." The enormous work which an infant must perform in learning basic enjoyable uses of himself can account in full for his great need for rest and sleep. A right view of infancy shows the mighty self-helpfulness which every baby must exert in order to struggle cheerfully through the heavy demands and trying ordeals which his earliest life puts upon him. The infant's observer tends to feel helpless and therefore quickly displaces this uncomfortable feeling upon his infant.

Just as this beginner educates himself (by self-growth)

to the function of binaural hearing or to the coordination of his eyes, so he exercises his learning process to develop his personal lessons of self-power as he lives them in *his* " mother " (or " nurse ") experiences. Every baby's mind thus creates his own mother personation living herself in such a way that the baby usually senses benefit for himself in creating this kind of (his) mother-living. Every infant *learns* (by living them) all of the self-activities which later on he comes to designate as his " mother," his father," and his " everyone " and " everything."

As in psychotherapy so in the learning process in general, it is not sufficient that the pupil learn by rote. Rote knowledge is the most superficial of all forms of knowledge. It involves the acknowledged mental dissociation of the learner from that which he learns. Unconscious self-knowledge is a most troublesome form of ignorance. As the insight of the psychotherapist can have nothing to do with the insight of the patient, so the knowledge of the teacher can have nothing to do with the knowledge of the pupil. The student's attention to his learning (living) *for its personal meaning* is the essence of hygienic education.

The only possible alternative to this definition of education (as inviolable self-activity) is its definition (however carefully disguised) as: authoritative manipulation of an uninformed mind by an informed mind. The latter orientation of inequality founded upon the " smarter than thou " pedagogical system is reminiscent of the " holier than thou " and " healthier than thou " authoritarian fallacies. Perceptive and consciously self-contained psychologist, C. K. Ogden, recorded in *The Meaning of Psychology*: " That the perception should be the key to the movements required to reproduce it and that the reproduction should often take place as a kind of completion of the whole process is not more mysterious than anything else that we do." [25]

## THE EDUCATOR

> Scientists have not greatly helped the world to humanize Science and socialize technology. But most tragic of all, *scientists have not done what is possible toward integrating the bodies of knowledge created by science into a unified interpretation of man, his place in nature, and his potentialities for creating the good society*. Instead, they are entombing us in dark and meaningless catacombs of learning.
>
> *Oliver L. Reiser*

The danger which lies in any personification of my very own selfness (such as "somebody else," "religion," "research," "society," "science," or whatever) is that such an imagined endowment of an abstraction with "external" life is, as a rule, maintained at the expense of the gratifying appreciation for (that much of) my own life, which gratification is essential for my health. Current trends in educator awareness are favorable to this self-development orientation, since it is becoming increasingly plain to see that traditional educational procedure (based upon the mind-withering illusions of "the teacher educating the pupil" and "the pupil being educated by the teacher") must be responsible for the innumerable danger signals coming from the educated. These humane protests have become progressively fearful through the centuries of formal schooling until now (with uncertain responsibility for atomic bombing) they are assuming the terrifying proportion of life annihilation.

"It is hardly too much to say that education is the largest word in the vocabulary of life." [26]

The kind of education which makes hot or cold war inevitable; which necessitates human misery by restricting conscious courage and cheer; which specifically trains for mental "disorder"—this education is the growth of personal knowledge which is not recognizable as self-knowledge. The pleasing illusion that one person can agree with another leads to the displeasing illusion that one can disagree with another. Thus, discordant ("disordered") mind begins.

It is all the more practical therefore that the educative process be accurately understood. In all humaneness, the truth needs to be firmly established, as soon as possible, that one person cannot and must not be held responsible for education of another person. This self-evident truth carries implications which dispel some of my dearest illusions. Thus, beginning with the mother who is most frequently miscalled "the first educator," it is only humanely decent that she be able to clear herself once and for all of any responsibility whatsoever with regard to the education (including training) of her infant and child. Once she can absolve herself of the (impossible) responsibility for developing her infant, she can then concentrate upon the (possible) responsibility for cultivating her own conscious integrity. *Fortunate is the infant who personates his loving mother by having her do all of her mothering as a conscious effort to help herself!*

Who is then the first educator? Who can it possibly be but each individual himself. Whoever first starts to educate himself, is properly entitled to the honor of calling himself the first educator. In every instance this title is properly conferred upon the sage of the womb, the newborn baby.

The following line of questioning now becomes practical. What is the most hazardous occupation of all? What labor, though it is truly the most dangerous, has the fewest safeguards? What line of work *appears* to be the safest, the least apt to require any daring or heroism, the farthest removed from the real threats and perils of the world? The experienced one's reply to each of the questions may be the same: the educator's. Excepting the parent, the teacher conducts his world's most critical work. Indeed responsibility for peace, as for war, can and must be placed at only one door, every human being's (self-) education.

What then is this ominous peril which every educator wittingly or unwittingly assumes? Fortunately it may be pinpointed: *the danger of obscuring human dignity by ignoring sound individuality.* The peace and progress of my whole world depend directly upon my ability to educate myself to observe it (my world) and take care of it as a going concern of my own life. Every blind spot in my self-observation also means that my pupil must grow as his own a teacher lacking that much of the essential ingredient of mental maturity, namely, conscious devotion to his own life's meaning.

The whole combination called " an education " exists nowhere except in the mind using it. Awarenes of that fact brings with it an increase of vitality and lucidity. *Self-insight (self-consciousness) associated with the mental genesis known as education animates the central principle of all human being, namely, the appreciation of life.* My actuality of *being* a life is anterior to my recognizing what I can *do* with it. However, my very worth as a person becomes clear to me only to the extent that, by finding what my life can do for me, I enable myself to place the true value upon my present living (all I ever have).

Sometimes it is difficult for me to be able to see that as long as I live all I *can* do is learn to help myself. *All of my living is really as therapeutic as it can be.* The daring dictum of Cervantes, " Give the devil his due," is wisdom not easily put to use, but for any and all getting on to further self-helpfulness it is essential that I credit myself with present self-helpfulness. Even if it does not look like help, Whatever I live *helps.* If I concentrate upon living myself as " feeling helpless," that view too is a human one and has its life-affirming meaning. My inability to see any of my living as helpful gives to that particular living an obsessive force which blocks further advance in self-helpfulness. All deception is compensation for unready self-insight, for the wandering of self-interest in the guise of unselfishness.

I derive great benefit from upholding my sense of esteem in any and all of my living, including my living of my " immaturities," " mistakes," and " failures,"—only thereby can I free myself from blindly persevering in that apparently ineffectual living. Rejected selfness behaves as a " rejected child " does, constantly seeking acceptance. My application of this specific self-insight reveals every one of my stumbling blocks as a stepping stone.

On account of the pressing and exacting necessities of my earliest home living, I had to help myself in many ways which certainly did not appear helpful at all under my later living of similar conditions. To illustrate, as an infant and child I had to help myself by protesting or by crying, sometimes without even realizing the helpfulness in such a complaint. However, no matter how I now carry on, once I can view each particular way with sustained self-respect as my present *only possible* effort to help myself, I then no longer restrict myself to its limited self-helpfulness.

White House conferences on education signalize growing official appreciation of the fact that a tyrant is educated to become a tyrant, a communist is educated to become a communist, a mature American citizen is educated to become a consciously self-governing individual, and so on. To this fine kind of appreciation may be added the all-powerful insight: Everyone can and must educate himself to become whatever he becomes. Any fateful poverty of this specific educational insight, whether in a first-grader or in a United Nation's educator, can be relieved by self-awareness, provided only that its wanter wills it.

The human being is wisest who consciously exercises most the sovereignty of his individual nature in his education of himself. Quite as Socrates stated it, " Man is the obstetrician of his own ego." Every powerful meaning of " Education " is subordinate to the individual *mind* (authority) originating it. In his classic essay, " Mechanistic Biology and the Religious Consciousness," Joseph Needham records this wisdom,

> . . . as far as mental life is concerned biochemistry and biophysics have no authority. The opinion, therefore, which seems to me to be most justifiable is that life in all its forms is the phenomenal disturbance created in the world of matter and energy when mind comes into it. Living

> matter is the outward and visible sign of the presence of mind, the splash made by the entry of mental existences into the sea of inert matter.[27]

(Bio-) physics and (bio-) chemistry are applied biology, —not the converse. To do justice to this view would resolve all (phantom) "mind-body" problems: *Everything is only and all about itself.* Mind can be accounted for only in terms (vocabulary) of mind; chemistry only in terms (vocabulary) of chemistry; physics, only in terms (vocabulary) of physics; and so on. Rudolf Carnap said it well, "*The logic of science is nothing other than* the logical syntax of the language of science." [28] Mixing categories, the displacement of an assertion which is certain for one word order to another word order, entails no end of mental trouble. Nowhere is it signalized by greater distress than by the indulgence of the illusion that one individual can (somehow) get at, or be gotten at, by another individual. The "extraneous" is *all* and *only* about the "extraneous."

In my life I see *every* production is a subjective one. I subjectively hypostatize (my) objectivity. "Again, the structure of language itself is an incarnation of the laws of thought; so much so, that Aristotle sought to determine the essential categories of thinking by an analysis of grammatical forms." [29] My every word, or combination of words, is all and only a use of my mind and *can never mean more than it is.* If I use my words validly for studying my mind, I may not attribute any word to that which I designate as "non-mental," for all that I can mean by "mind" is all and only about itself. Such a study may be accurately called "psychology." If I use my words validly for studying my mind's application to any (imagined) " non-mental " discipline (any of my investigation of my " physical " world) , I may not attribute any word to that which I designate as mental, for all that I can mean by " non-mental " is all and only about itself. The latter kind of study may be accurately called " applied psychology." Noteworthy is the fact that these dispositions of my (one) mental system do not involve me in any kind of philosophical " dualism," " psychophysical parallelism," " interactionism," or any kind of " system " other than my human system. Attempting admixtures of my psychology and my applied psychology necessarily produces confusion. " Mental states are first broken from the only connection in which they have any meaning; and then are mistaken for the ground of their own condition." [30] Mind-consciousness (self-insight) and materialism can grow only in inverse proportion. I define my study of psychology as the systematic cultivation of my self-observation. In his " Ode to Psyche," Keats visualized conscious-mindedness clearly.

> O latest born and loveliest vision far
> Of all Olympus' faded hierarchy
> . . . . . .

## HOW SELF-INSIGHT GROWS ITSELF

> The soul selects her own society,
> Then shuts the door;
> On her divine majority
> Obtrude no more.
>
> *Emily Dickinson*

When the process of *noting* selfness does once start it soon stops unless it makes itself start again. I must *work* for my consent, my will, that it be free to start again.

I am loving and helping myself whenever I indulge any delusion that I am loved and helped by "someone else." I have to "save my face" with this delusion if I have not developed sufficient self-esteem to see my own selfness in my beloved. Nowhere is the delusional living of "otherness" more costly than in "*falling* in love,"—in my cultivating my love for my loved one at the expense of lowering rather than raising my sense of self-esteem. Freud saw this risk clearly, specifying that "an actual happy love corresponds to the primal condition" in which object-love and ego-love cannot be distinguished.

Before I cultivated the art of getting my own attention (by practicing the hard lesson of catching sight of myself) I was not able to be quite bright about my own life. I treated myself, including my fellowman, as a means rather than as an end. Taking the trouble of focusing my interest upon my way of growing myself (my continuing I-hood) is the technique by which my mind accustoms itself to elevating itself. Every moment of my life is potentially a new opportunity for me to observe my dynamic dimension. Thus far, I have found this man's job of growing of my self-insight to provide "the last word" in freedom, naturalness, sensibility, perceptiveness, reasonableness, resoluteness, diligence, wisdom, innocence, sentiment, and sublimity. For me, the "well educated mind" is the (clearly recognized) self-begotten one which has discovered the practicality of valuing insight (mind-consciousness, the sense of personal identity in whatever is being lived) most highly. The possessor of this mind does not, as Peer Gynt did, seem to find his ideal self in the imagination of another,—but instead in his own mind's "fair and immortal children" (Plato).

I succeeded in resolving dread associated with my heroic solipsistic position ("I am my own all") only by strengthening my appreciation of myself through exploring (and thus dispelling) my illusion that "anyone else" could live any of my self-appreciation or self-depreciation for me. I achieved great mental economy by observing that my fellow man's admiration could only be his own (acknowledged or unacknowledged) admiration for himself. Molière's play hero was greatly pleased with himself to learn that he had been talking prose all of his life. Everyone who discovers that all of his talk has always been about his own life enjoys incomparable self-satisfaction. *In interiore homine habitat veritas,* soliloquized Saint Augustine. To recognize that I can be only self-pleased, or self-displeased,—that is self-enlightenment. "Union must be inward," said Emerson, "Union must be ideal in actual individualism."

What technique did I use to make this arrangement with myself (for observing myself in my unifications)? The technique of *increasing my wish for this kind of development,—my wanting it and wanting it harder and harder until I could no longer do (be) without it.* Choosing to live in the selfward direction, self-felt living, is the only possible escape from the mind-obscuring "external world" predicament and the troublesome subject *vs.* object enigma. I am only selfish about it, but I can scarcely bear to see my fellow man steadily looking at his world as if it is not all his own subjective creation. All that any man really can want is himself, and his *conscious* discontent is desirable until he succeeds in finding himself.

Again, how did I learn how to grow self-insight? How did I learn to embrace self-consciousness and renounce auto-hypnosis? By what "technique" do I free myself from my dependence upon my "illusional externalities"? How do I discover for myself the Why's and Wherefore's with which I displace my own (self-) meaning of consciousness and thereby live *as if* I can be "out of my mind"? How do I grow the strength to renounce my ease with this mental dislocation and my corresponding neglect of my allness? How do I show myself that individuality is the basic law of my being? These questions presuppose that *I wish* (will) to learn to live myself consciously. However, this wish must ever be highlighted, not taken for granted. First I must hunger and thirst for that life prospect and remain painfully conscious of my starvation and dryness (lack of enthusiasm, of radiant vitality, of spiritual fervor) until I help myself to relieve my life with awareness. Until then I may say with Browning, "man is not Man yet." Plato revealed, "Whosoever seeks a thing knows that which he seeks for in a general notion; else how shall he know it when he has found it?"

Making my consciousness work is a matter of having it report only my selfness,—in every instance a daring development requiring and augmenting my human hardihood. Repairing, or "fixing up," my consciousness so that it works accurately for me (by always manifesting to me my own living) is my most important health problem. Not by musing but by mighty hard work must I solve it. If I wish to be as one of self-insight I must live as one of self-insight lives. One's own biological force plays the only role in human individuality,—whether one sees psychology in physics or sees physics in psychology. Matthew Arnold wrote of his personal experience:

Bounded by themselves, and unregardful
In what state God's other works may be,
In their own tasks all their powers pouring,
These attain the mighty life you see.

Truth appears in both proverbs: " Where there is no vision the people perish " and " Where there is a will there is a way." Technique (strategy, tactics) is useful but can never substitute for incentive and intention in serving to clear my mental vision, to exercise my awareness of my life's worth. Certainly, pursuit of the continuous production of new self-valuation is a vocation which requires the motivation of sincere, earnest, loyal, vigilant (self-) devotion. " Intuitive insight, made use of, leads to further insight, but an attitude of conceit may hold up the development of further insight, by finding sufficient satisfaction in admiration of that already achieved." [31]

With *my* raw life-stuff grows self-consciousness. With unobstructed self-consciousness grows conscious self-love. With revered self-love grows self-will. With honored self-will grows self-help. Acknowledged self-help enables me to avoid my misleading myself by a consciousness which shows its inaccuracy by reporting " not-self." How do I know? In the same way I know anything: I experienced it. Before that, I had studied the classic records of the uses of " inner experience " but only the testimony of my very own experience had any power of conviction for me. There is no unearned " received " self-consciousness. Somewhat as Whitman declared it, I must work the gum from my own eyes. " You must habit yourself to the dazzle of the light, and of every moment of your life."

" May you live all the days of your life," wished Dean Swift. Only by practicing the conduct of conscious self-development have I strengthened and healed my mind; only by practicing the conduct of unconscious self-development have I troubled my mind. Self-possession is the product of the cultivation of mine-ness.

What passes for undesirable "selfishness" is really nothing but narrowly restricted selfishness. My narrow "selfishness" towards any of my living is cured only by my *extending my sense of selfishness* so that it sees itself in that which it formerly disowned. Self-love cannot be freely expressed except where there is conscious (recognizable) self-knowledge. "Unselfish" love is unconscious self-love. My love is as non-dual as is my self. Increasing my conscious self-knowledge extends my self-love and, thereby, *my interest in living.* "Men do not die! they kill themselves!" said Seneca.

Love, wisdom, and the power of self-perceptibility grow together. I must work out my own worthwhileness of living based only upon my own sense of benefit. Wisdom breeds worldliness recognizable as self-worldliness. Observing my identity in my all is essential for my full appreciation of the sanative truth of such divine humanities as Existence, Consciousness, Equality, Freedom, Justice, Love, Life, Nature, Happiness, Health, Peace, Interest, Help, Work, Wholeness (Impartiality), and Meaning itself. Anaxagoras said, "All things were in chaos when Mind arose and made order."

I ask myself, What do I regard as one primary self-insight? I reply, My recognition that my mind is neglected and oppressed (ill). *Without this insight I cannot have any conscious motivation for attending to and freeing (healing) my mind.*

Every adult feels keenly the absence of a certain specific

attitude towards his life which he enjoyed as a child. For many years of my professional life I strove vainly to recover this particular life-orientation which I had forgotten while "growing up." It seemed to me that every other "grown-up" was also engaged in a similar kind of blind searching. Finally I discovered what this desideratum was. *It was the consciousness of my innocence,*—of my feeling of wholesomeness and freedom from life-depreciation. Innocence is the ear-mark of *conscious* individuality, the specific feeling of freedom from (illusional) "externals."

I had often heard childhood referred to as "the paradise of innocence," without making the connection that my enjoyment of my sense of *innocence* was what was sorely missing in my life. This connection once made, the invigorating truth of certain educational directives of my own childhood then began to make sense to me, "Out of the mouths of babes," "Unless ye become as little children," "Of such are the kingdom," "Born again," "A little child shall lead them." Freud, healing hour of consciousness of his mankind, not only saw and recorded this truth anew but made it accessible upon a scientific basis.

After getting on the track of all of the joy and freedom of living (which I had been forfeiting by neglecting the truth of my innocence) I began to realize that formerly I had to suffer monitory guilt feeling (the sense of wrongdoing) rather than enjoy innocence, as long as I persisted blindly in relying upon my (temporarily useful) self-deceptions: self-denial, unselfishness, self-sacrifice, self-unconsciousness, (all negative meanings).

My only possible answer to a fact of such recognized potency as this, was to make it the object of my most careful study. Out of this scientific labor I worked up a properly respectful appreciation of my ability to forget distressing experience as being a helpful anaesthetic permitting me (during traumatic experience) to preserve my sense of identity at least, even though on a limited scale. I saw how I succeeded in staving off complete demoralization (the mental regression of "going all to pieces") by practicing self-unconsciousness (amnesia) for overwhelmingly painful (traumatic) portions of my living.

Later on I saw also my need to cultivate the conscious self-endurance which only could enable me to begin to grow equal to myself, to the extent of seeing that I am my dislikes as much as I am my likes and that I am my "not-I" (repressed) living as much as I am my "I" (consciously affirmed) living. Since living is growing, since living is learning in an ever surviving sequence, I cannot well afford to sleep upon my laurels of self-insight, but must *work* at keeping (not forgetting) the feeling of equality in my evolving self-world.

The most I can say of anything is: It works well. My aim for myself is to be able to work well. Osler considered work to be the solvent of unhappiness in his essay on his "magic" word: work. My own experience has demonstrated that my greatest life happiness is associated directly with my work capacity. Inhibition of my ability to exert myself is distressing. Facilitation of my ability to employ myself is satisfying. A mature infant, child or adult loves to work diligently to the extent that he is aware that his life is all his own. By "mature" I mean: consciously a complete individual.

Everyone's theory and practice of psychotherapy directly demonstrates the way in which he takes care of his own mind. St. Augustine described the growth of his self-insight as follows:

> Such was the story of Pontitianus. But Thou, O Lord, whilst he was speaking, didst turn me towards myself, taking me from behind my back, where I had placed myself while unwilling to exercise self-scrutiny; and Thou didst set me face to face with myself, . . . And if I sought to turn my gaze away from myself, he continued his narrative, and Thou again opposedst me unto myself and thrustedst me before my own eyes, that I might discover my iniquity and hate it. I had known it, but acted as though I knew it not,—winked at it, and forgot it.

How to learn so that my learning is observed by me as developing my " subject matter " as my own mental power, needs to be learned itself. It is my teacher's function to present his own learning as having all and only this meaning (the systematic conscious cultivation of his mind). It is a chief characteristic of a mind undisciplined with its own consciousness to ignore its events which do not appear to be one body acting upon, or acted upon by, another body. Primitives are prone to these " ideas of influence " and " ideas of reference " which characterize the oppressed mind.

In one of his novels the genius Flaubert had two of his characters (Bouvard and Pécuchêt) work on this problem of How to grow self-insight. Each read that the goal of psychology is to introspect upon the facts which take place " in the bosom of the self." " And for a fortnight, after breakfast regularly, they hunted about at random in their minds, hoping to make notable discoveries, and made none and were much surprised." Little wonder that this technique revealed to each one only that which he was ready to see, for the kind of sight-seeing which is insightful involves a modification of the organ of mental vision itself.

Each new insight changes the boundaries of my seeing self, of my mind's own eye. As *I* grow insight my I, itself, undergoes modification which enables my increased self-observation. For insightful living, " I " (as subject) must live " me " (as object) with essential sameness (personal identity) perceptible in the whole operation, so that my sense of my wholeness is not lost anywhere in my process of perceiving or of being perceived. Otherwise feelings of inequality and heterogeneity will occur (instead of feelings of equality and homogeneity) and my " I " living will seem inconsistent (hence incompatible) with my *me* living. " After all 'I' *is* psychology. Without 'I' the science of human psychology must inevitably become a subordinate branch of general physiology." [32]

## THE GROWTH OF SELF–INSIGHT IN SCIENTIFIC RESEARCH

> The scientific investigation of nature strives to recognize the universal in every particular, so that at last it may come nearer to the source of all things.
>
> *Goethe*

The only way in which I can observe the true meaning of any part of my scientific research is by my unifying observation that *it* is a particular of my own general living, that my every scientific datum is a particular individuation of my general individuality. " Impersonal observation " is a contradiction of terms.

While self-consciousness presides, my value judgments and reasonings become evident as rationalizations and paranoid constructions. Self-consciousness elucidates the allness of oneness and dispenses with multiplicity, divisibility and relativity of any kind. Only my I-feeling can liberate my human mind from the yoke of every authority but its own. Only it can disclose inequality, injustice and despotism of every kind as helpful signs of (individual) mental imbalance.

All meaning is *personal* only. All of my understanding is my seeing my personal selfness is what I " understand." Meaning, itself, is the basic unit of any given mind and, in its totality, it comprises all of mindfulness. Of all of my mind's meanings, impulse, or wish, seems to be most elemental. The comprehensive meaning of my human life, itself, is that it is entirely and only my own personal experience. I wish to work up the power to see that its every meaning is all and only about me. Socrates deemed the unexamined life unworthy of man.

The dissociation of man and his life (his living of his world) is his only mental trouble. In no other way than selfly can I conceive my human (including physicianary) worth forcibly enough. Seeing my soul (self) as my all is the law of sanity; quite as ignoration of my soul (self) is the law of insanity. In every generalization the individual is ignored, unless he is clearly *noticed* as the generalizer.

*My health of mind varies directly with my recognition of its wealth.* I can never see all of myself at a time any more than I can look with all of myself at a time. The production of self-insight is piecework. Technically stated, a strong well ego is one which is observed and appraised as intact by its possessor. I am, my all is, entirely my life. Furthermore, I have discovered the source of my mental health and strength to lie in living this appreciation and, thus, appreciating my living. I have no greater human helpfulness than my difficultly developed ability to make a virtue of necessity.

Every scientist justly prides himself upon his tolerance of " Whatever is," and the *idea* of the exclusively personal significance of even his scientific world is no exception. Whatever is, exactly is; whatever is, extremely is. I am exactly and extremely my own " Whatever is." With this insight I can escape the self-trap which Whitehead aptly calls " The fallacy of misplaced concreteness." Each reader who wishes may comfort himself with Henri Poincaré's assertion, " These two propositions, ' the external world exists,' or ' it is more convenient to suppose that it exists,' have one and the same meaning." Certain it is that each of these propositions consists of the sameness of which its creator is constituted.

Consciousness is focused attention; it is my mind's act of self-observation (self-interest). My living is always a proper object for this fresh study. Studied attention to all of my experiences as being entirely and only my personal life-theme is pure scientific realism. My own humanity is my only " knowable," and whatever I live is my only scientific province. My mind is where I experience appreciation of my individuality, and even the crudest working plan of my mental nature and needs is already an incalculable benefit.

Both deduction (seeing the universal in the particular) and induction (seeing the particular in the universal) involve the free use of my speculation. Speculation activates my mental power of imagination, the freedom of which is most essential for my diffusion of my awareness that my humanity is all there is to my living. Tyndall described imagination as " the mightiest instrument of the physical discoverer."

My most clever defenses against sufficient learning are, " That is not true," " I heard that before," and, " I know that already." By means of each of these claims I can avoid the exertion required for making my knowledge evident as my self-knowledge. I can test the reality strength of my knowledge by observing the degree to which I can (1) value it as self-knowledge, and (2) enjoy free access to its use. I can know thoroughly only that which I can will to use freely.

My self-flattering view-point, " I should know better," is always a comforting blinder obscuring my need to exert myself further (stretch my self-tolerance) in order to be able to " know better." Emily Dickinson beautifully described her mind's problems of self-toleration,

> The soul has bandaged moments
> When too appalled to stir.

and

> The truth must dazzle gradually
> Or every man be blind.

If my life were not both difficultly and easily lived I could never realize my potential manpower. From all of her experience in self-tolerance, wonderful Helen Keller observed, " Toleration is the greatest gift of the mind; it requires the same effort of the brain that it takes to balance oneself on a bicycle."

All human excitation, that is, all vivid individual experience, sensory and motor, functions as a succedaneum for self-consciousness. To feel glad, or sad, or angry, or dispassionate, or whatever, is to feel self that much and to minister gropingly to the precious love of life.

## THE PHYSICIAN'S SELF-INSIGHT UNDERLIES HIS ART OF MEDICINE

> Men had lived, and perhaps lived many thousand years, before one of them hit upon the thought that life could be an art.
>
> *Wieland*

" A physican who is also a philosopher is as a god," said Hippocrates. Only insofar as I have *consciously* purposeful access to my mental power can I scientifically estimate my mind as being powerful. This strict prerequisite explains fully the neglect of the role of the allness of mind in human affairs. The truth-borne need for shifting the mind's focus from " worldly knowledge " to self-consciousness, once courageously recognized, leads through this energetic toil to a spontaneous growth in free self-interest, a new estimate of conscious human individuality, and a determination to cultivate manifest self as the foundation of all understanding.

Said Charles-Edward A. Winslow of Yale University School of Medicine, " Not disease prevention but health promotion must be the watchword of the future. ' Health ' is something much more than merely staying out of a coffin." And, " What we must develop in the future is constructive medicine, in which the center of interest is the individual and his maximum potentialities." Conscious living is the ultimate in hygienic workmanship.

The discovery of the *art of life* was the birth of philosophy, recognized early as " medicine for the soul," as remedy for the " fever of life." Cicero maintained Nature to be the best guide of life and claimed that no one could fail who guided himself with Nature. The apparent contradiction, Nature *vs.* Art, dissipates itself with the realization that Art is entirely made up of Nature. Owen Meredith sagely noted, " Art is Nature made by Man." However, as Ben Jonson observed, " Art hath an enemy called ignorance." My ignorance of my ignorance is my hidden need.

Medicine, as the strengthening and healing Art, prospers insofar as each physician uses his Art entirely as a refinement of his reliance upon *vis medicatrix naturae,* that is, upon his patient's unitive ability to heal himself. If I try to function as a physician, without as complete as possible a study of what my patient is already doing (naturally) to cure himself by means of his helpful signs and symptoms,—then my patient may simply come to add his physician to all of his other complaints. " Meddle " and " Medical " are mutually exclusive terms.

The race is not to the swift but to the one going toward the right goal. As Santayana defined it, " Fanaticism consists in redoubling your effort when you have lost your aim." In all considerations educational (including medical) the right goal is at the end of full realization that all help is self-help. Every patient lives all that he understands to be *his* physician; every physician lives all that he understands to be *his* patient. Insight upon this state of medical affairs, existence-consciousness, may well be described as Comprehensive Medicine, as Medical Consciousness. When Georg Groddeck wrote, " The Doctor's chief danger is Hybris," he apparently had in mind the ease with which every patient's soul-evolving powers of healing may be disregarded. As long as there is life there remains the potential for new reaches of excellence.

The art of medicine is based upon the fine appreciation

of the natural meanings of individuality in medical study and practice. In medical work any schism of humaneness and science is not natural. May such artificial division of human nature be abandoned. Technique involves humaneness always. In *A History of Medical Psychology* (written in collaboration with George W. Henry) Gregory Zilboorg summarized: " The history of psychiatry is essentially the history of humanism. Every time humanism has diminished or degenerated into mere philanthropic sentimentality, psychiatry has entered a new ebb. Every time the spirit of humanism has arisen, a new contribution to psychiatry has been made." [33]

I once made the statement that my clinical work-up of every so-called " villain " always revealed him as a hero, as a desperate man driving himself fiercely to wild efforts (an heroic struggle) to help himself. The question was raised, How can you regard a world criminal as a hero? My reply was, *Only by the greatest effort can I do so.* It is the hardest kind of *work* which enables me to see a so-called world-criminal as victimizing himself by the very kind of world he lives. To recover my mental balance enough to undergo the tremendous exertion of seeing my most vicious reprobate as the understandable world of distress which he is, it helps me to realize that, of all persons, he is the one I would not like to have to be, that his life is the one I would most hate to have to live. The life-oppressing alternative to working up this insightful living of my tormenting malefactor is to devote my own life to the living of bitterness, retaliation, illusions of " wrong."

A similar extension of my insight is most practical for me as I view my torn and mangled patient, and turn to his bleeding and fractured body with love, rather than with dislike and aversion. A " horribly " injured child suffers extreme need for its accepting *approving* mother. Rejection of his wounds means rejection of him, and adds to his demoralization. The physician in the emergency room must develop this reach of clinical sense (self-consciousness) in order to recognize and practice the precious life-saving lessons inherent in " accidents " and " illnesses."

Vital functions are so many ways of expressing the personal meanings of existence. Visceral processes constitute body language expressing life energy in its balanced existence, mediating the forces which tend to continue and terminate life. Sang Homer, " Fate gives the wound, and man is born to bear." All of the mind's activities appear to be carried out by excitations which modify physiological processes. Sir Thomas Browne deplored ignoration of the ensouled body, " To devolve the honour of the principal agent upon the instrument, which, if with reason we may do, then let our hammers rise up and boast that they have built our houses, and our pens receive the honor of our writings." A body without a mind is dead. Every organ ordeal is a mental ordeal, in the profound sense that it threatens life itself. Stated Swedenborg, " Whatever there is in the mind is in the brain and from the brain, in the body, according to the order of its parts. So a man writes his life in his physique." Commenting upon such life lessons, Dr. Nolan D. C. Lewis adds, " May I prophesy that also the psychiatrist and the pathologist should eventually be able to make a similar discovery, but one that can be utilized to the benefit of the living patient? " For instance, " What is cancer of an organ saying for its possessor? " or, " What is nephritis expressing of the psychology of its owner? " and so on.

Unless the material involved be mental material, there can be no "materialist." "Materialism," referring to non-mental material, is, as the negation indicates, disowned (repressed) idealism. My "materialistic" fellow man is a "materialist" by virtue of the fact that he disowns his "external world" as being entirely his own living of it. In technical terms, any part of my life of which I say, "It is not I," becomes a part of my life which I must live "in transference" (unconsciously, involuntarily, repetitiously, anesthetically,—quite as a foreign body). All of my "transference behavior" is the product of the living of my own mental powers *as if* they were "externalized." By definition, *every materialist (to the extent that he claims consciousness of "external data") must forego the benefits of his self-consciousness.*

A mind that has partially lost itself has great difficulty distinguishing magnanimity from megalomania, and often gives vent to the question, "What is the difference between calling your whole world your own and claiming that your life is wonderful, and the psychotic patient's delusions of grandeur and pathological euphoria?" A megalomanic patient *is* reality oriented insofar as he sees himself as wonderful. His trouble stems from the fact that he does not see *enough* of himself as wonderful. Thus, he does not attribute wonderfulness to his "others." His euphoria appears to derive from his uninhibited use of himself within the restricted limits of his conscious personal identity. He does not love himself too much, he just does not love enough of himself.

A most practical helpfulness for any and every kind of human ordeal is the patient's mobilization of his manpower, the furthering of the concentration of the forces of self-interest, self-helpfulness and self-appreciation. The achievement (learning) of this kind of health organization is specifically a psychotherapeutic one. Two principles are to be duly noted in every health ordeal:

(1) Presence of mental distress rules in anatomical structural change.

(2) Presence of organic structural change rules in mental distress.

Regardless of the nature of his health stress (whether it be an acute or chronic infection, a localized or generalized disease process, or an injury) each patient has his own individual psychology about it. He uses each kind of organ stress in a way which is unique for him as a person, depending entirely upon its meaning for him. Every person's health vicissitudes of any and every kind are all and only about his very own life,—critical developments of profound meaning for his life-orientation, biological events developing his personal system of psychology. The physician can have nothing to do with the patient; the patient can have nothing to do with the physician; the disease entity can have nothing to do with either one. Each (physician, patient, or disease entity) is all and only about itself. Each is its own all.

The meaning of any organ of the body is certainly not limited to its physiological role. Whatever mentality his organ has developed for a patient represents a factor which functions forcibly whenever there is organ stress. To illustrate, no two patients have developed the same set of forceful meanings for the kidney and its function, but each one has grown for himself his own characteristic life meanings of this kind.

## SUMMARY

> Does the newly proposed view remove more difficulties, require fewer assumptions, and present more consistency with observed facts than that which it seeks to supersede? If so, the philosopher will adopt it, and the world will follow the philosopher—after many days.
>
> *Grove*

The Leo M. Franklin Memorial Lectures are devoted to the advancement of the ideal of humaneness, of loving appreciation of human life. I submit, The law governing the development of humaneness is: conscious living of one's world as constituted of one's own human being.

For my lecture series I chose the exposition of the one and only way in which I have found it possible to study and practice humaneness: by laboriously extending my awareness of *my* human being and thereby observing that *my* world is my own *human* life's creation. What is constructive, or destructive, for *my* world is by definition constructive, or destructive, for me. Any other reporting of my senses misrepresents my own life to me.

I have grown the strength of mind to expect my reader to find quickly some kind of a school of philosophy within which to enclose his Dorsey,—" intuitionism," ' solipsism," " neo-vitalism," " intellectualism," " individualism," or whatever. My only comment about that is, " Fine, he is helping himself by so doing." My truth, however, is that my every school of philosophy, psychology, education, and so on, belongs to me,—not I to it.

Knowledge exists *only* as evidence of a life, as a sign of a human being. Scientific knowledge is founded upon observation. Every observation is the observer's own mental product. Occam noted, everything real is individual. Observing individuality only, in my every view, that is sanity. Each scientific datum is a human existent. Appreciation of this truth (self-insight) is mind-healing and mind-strengthening. Certainly I may make many important " scientific discoveries " with never a consideration for the mind-helpful truth that each is all and only my self-activity. However, the substance of all of my science, quite as the content of all of my reality, is always made up of *my* life's creativity,—not of its oblivion.

Scientific discovery (learning) is ordinarily described in terms of psychic action, but it consists of the only action of which a human being is capable, namely, his living. It is the awareness of the possession of present life which makes life consciously valuable. Only immediate living of my human selfhood can mean anything to me and can furnish me with any and all of my meanings. Humanizing my scientific data by observing they are life of my life enlarges my available stockpile of self-possession and sanatizes my research living. Only my self-conscious scientific work can be sufficiently conscionable. To ignore this epistemological premise is to make mental trouble for myself as a scientist.

My educational living can only exercise and develop my human being. Realization of this fact develops a new conception of the value of human individuality. Nevertheless, I can *appear* to myself to live all that I call " Education " with an " impersonal " (" not-self " and " externality ") orientation to it, thereby depriving myself of my humanizing self-awareness. So long as this mind-anaesthetizing and mind-paralyzing theory prevails I shall be giving myself painful warnings that I am hypnotizing myself to understimate my worth. My all-important consideration is: The presence or absence of my self-awareness is all that makes the difference between my free mental life (health) and my oppressed mental life (illness). For me the end of learning is the enjoyment of my own self-fulfillment, the life-satisfying cultivation of my manpower, the happy realization of my potential. I see learning as having the same kind of end for each of my fellow creatures. As William A. White declaimed, "Certainly I am sure that how we think about things is of as much importance as what we think about them."

If I live myself without *conscious* self-culture I provide myself with such danger signals as "sickness," or "accidents," or some such indications of life-dissatisfaction about the neglect. The pleasure and pain of my satisfaction and dissatisfaction cannot be efficient monitors except insofar as I can recognize them as my own self's counselors. Any of my knowledge of advantage and disadvantage is of limited and scattered force if it lacks this self-reference. As Hippocrates recorded, "Nature is the physician of diseases," and I need to have the powers of my human nature accessible for my adequate self-helpfulness.

My life happiness, *aviditas vitae,* is the sensation I create by the free use of my manpower, by my renunciation of all of my "yokes of authority." The signal of inhibition of self-use is unhappiness, *taedium vitae.* Inhibition of my free use of my self-consciousness deprives me of the happiness of a man of peace and inflicts me with the unhappiness of a man of war.

Human life is ever *new,* admirable, wonderful, astonishing,—and it is easily understandable that I live it in varying degrees of stupor (self-unconsciousness) to the extent that I have not worked up my intention to see and feel my equality in it. Self-consciousness always illumines; only self-unconsciousness dazzles. The essence and charm of the naive consist in that it is obviously native to the individual, free of the pretense of being acquired.

Milton sang it: "The mind is its own place,"—and respect for that truth supports all other truth. My powerful resistances to "change for the better" are healthful expressions of self-possession, of my declared unreadiness for therapeutic ambitions other than my own. In self-defense against sudden demands that I grow more self-insight than I have, I must often rely upon one of my most powerful prescriptions for my authoritarian fellowman's importunity, namely, "I shall be pleased to consider it (whatever it may be)."

For the mind disciplined with the truth of self-helpfulness, the growth of self-insight also requires great mental exertion. It is easily avoided as extremely hard work. Nevertheless, without this specific hard work I have been unable to fulfill myself, to complete my appreciation of my life. It is only through doing this difficult work that I have cultivated that mental hardihood which I possess.

A most grievous complication of this work (of discovering where my experience takes place) has been my language, ill fitted to the task of describing all of my living as being only my own. My learning to speak was too much by rote, that is, without recognizing myself as the creator of each word, including all of its meaning. Thus, I used words which I could not see clearly as naming my own self-expressions, as if they did not apply only to myself. I increased my vocabulary at the cost of decreasing my self-insight and self-esteem. C. K. Ogden reported, "Language, in fact, is not only a means by which we hide our thoughts from other people; it is a veil which helps to hide our own lives from ourselves." To prevent my (verbally) "going out of my mind" so very consistently, I now sprinkle my vocabulary freely with "my" and "mine," renounce plurals as much as I can, and otherwise activate word-consciousness which helps me to make myself conspicuous to myself.

*Human individuality is not possibly isolable.* The term "isolation" is not applicable to an *all.* Totality has no "outside-ness." The term "plurality" only *appears* to overlook the truth of individuality. Every seeming "plurality," such as "group" or "many," is an instance of only one particular taking a quantitative form.

Disturbance of my equanimity warns me that my living (experience) is stretching my (conscious) self-tolerance beyond its established limits and, therefore, that I must either quit such experience or continue it at the risk of all of the distress and dangers associated with self-rejection.

My whole individuality is never accessible to me for my conscious disposition of it. Thus, I cannot do, or refrain from doing, anything as a conscious whole being. I can neither speak for, or to, all of myself. My pride and joy, my conscious living, is always only a part-act of the whole movement of my being. For instance, I cannot really suicide in the sense that all of me chooses to end its living as a conscious act. What is called "suicide" is always really death which is incidental to the carrying out of a delusion that one part of a person, his conscious self, is capable of representing his whole life. It is by means of my exercising my self-consciousness that I safeguard my natural life and natural death, avoiding my killing myself. It is even a helpful epitaph, " Here lies a man who thought the world of himself, thereby doing himself a world of good."

In his *Physics: The Elements,* N. R. Campbell noted:

> Ultimately the conclusion cannot be avoided that other persons (if anyone cares to express it so) are merely inventions of my own mind, and that their judgments are my judgments. My bitterest opponent is as much a creation of my own imagination as my most faithful disciple. Of course these statements sound absurd when they are expressed, but that is because language is incompetent to express what I mean without distortion. . . . Nearly all my active life is based on the assumption that I am one of others, but times must come when I retire into myself and force myself to recognise that the assumption is not true. And this truth is of course relative truth; it cannot possibly be expressed or comprehended by anyone else—if there were anyone else to comprehend it. To attempt to express the truth immediately leads to an inextricable tangle of inconsistencies. But if I am charged with them, I reply to myself, These inconsistencies are part of me; how can I be inconsistent with myself? Or in a wiser mood I hold my peace.[34]

Of " externality " Havelock Ellis said, " We can never solve the so-called world-riddle because what seem riddles to us are merely the contradictions we have ourselves created. We make our own world; when we make it awry we can remake it approximately truer. . . . Man lives by imagination."

Ever since I have grown sufficient self-insight to realize the *allness* of my personal existence I have discovered that it is from this realization that my life, itself, derives its fullest meaning. With this kind (degree) of self-realization, I have marveled without end at the profundity and sublimity of that ancient account: "God said unto Moses, I am that I am."

Lastly, for all of this expression of my convictions, based directly upon self-evidence which only I can witness, Alexander's just answer holds true. When Parmenio said to him, "I would accept the offer of Darius if I were Alexander," the prince replied, "So would I if I were Parmenio."

# *References*

## INTRODUCTION

1. *Freedom is the Right to Choose: An Inquiry into the Battle for the American Future* (Boston, 1950), p. 181.
2. *Emotion and the Education Process* (Washington, D. C., 1938), p. 156.

## IV. Goethe's Conception of Individuality and Personality

Citations from Goethe's writings are usually from *Goethes sämtliche Werke,* Jubiläums-Ausgabe (40 vols., Stuttgart u. Berlin, 1902-07. Abbreviated: *JA.*) There are occasional references to the so-called Weimar-Ausgabe, *Goethes Werke* (Weimar, 1887-1912). (Abbreviated: *WA.*) Where editions of Goethe's writings and conversations are cited, volume numbers are given in Arabic figures; divisions of the Weimar-Ausgabe are indicated by Roman numerals.

Translations by Hermann J. Weigand are from *Goethe: Wisdom and Experience* (abbreviated: *CW.*), selected by Ludwig Curtius, translated and edited with an introduction by Hermann J. Weigand (New York, 1949).

Translations from *Faust* are from J. F. L. Raschen, *Goethe's Faust* (Ithaca, 1949). All other English translations are mine unless otherwise indicated.

H. A. B.

1. See Arnold Bergstraesser (ed.), *Goethe and the Modern Age: The International Convocation at Aspen, Colorado, 1949* (Chicago, 1949).
2. *Wilhelm Meisters Wanderjahre,* 3. Buch, 13. Kapitel, *JA,* 20:190.
3. *Maximen u. Reflexionen,* No. 502 (*Wanderjahre*), see Robert Petsch (ed.), *Goethes Werke,* Kleine Ausgabe (Leipzig, n. d.), 7:347.
4. *Johann Wolfgang Goethe: Gedenkausgabe d. Werke, Briefe u. Gespräche,* ed. Ernest Beutler, 22 (Zürich, 1949): 388. See also *Goethes Gespräche,* ed. Woldemar Freiherr vs. Biedermann (Leipzig, 1889), 2:27-28.
5. *JA,* 2:229.

6. *Faust,* lines 11288-91. For translation, see Edwin H. Zeydel, *Goethe, the Lyrist* (Chapel Hill, 1955), p. 171.

7. Karl Jaspers, *Unsere Zukunft und Goethe* (Zürich, 1949), p. 43.

8. Barker Fairley, *A Study of Goethe* (London, 1947), p. 269.

9. Regarding the fundamental importance of distinguishing between the man and the artist Goethe, see Lienhard Bergel, "Croce as a Critic of Goethe," *Comparative Literature,* I (Fall, 1949), 349-59.

10. See Stanley Kunitz, "American Poetry's Silver Age," in *Harper's Magazine,* CCXIX (October, 1959), 178-79.

11. See Friedrich Nietzsche, *The Use and Abuse of History,* trans. Adrian Collins (New York, 1949).

12. From *Götzendämmerung* (*Twilight of the Idols*). See *Portable Nietzsche,* ed. Walter Kaufmann (New York, 1954), p. 553.

13. Karl Jaspers, as cited, p. 12. For a similar statement by Jakob Grimm, a contemporary of Goethe, see Heinrich Amelung, *Goethe als Persönlichkeit,* I (München, 1914), v.

14. *Feuillets d'Automne* (Paris, 1949). Cited in the New York *Times,* October 2, 1949.

15. See Friedrich Bruns, "Goethe in America," *Stechert-Hafner Book News,* IV (September, 1949), 1-4; also H. S. White, "Goethe und Amerika," *Goethe—Jahrbuch,* V (1884), 219 ff., and "Briefwechsel zwischen Goethe und Amerikanern," *Goethe—Jahrbuch,* XXV (1904), 3.

16. "Introduction to Goethe" (review), *Nation and Athenaeum,* January 12, 1929, p. 527.

17. Karl Shapiro, "T. S. Eliot: The Death of Literary Judgment," *Saturday Review,* February 27, 1960, pp. 12-17. For an evaluation of Eliot's attitude toward Goethe, see Robert L. Beare, "T. S. Eliot and Goethe," *Germanic Review,* XXVIII (December, 1953), 243-53.

18. "Two Poets" (review), *Bookman* (London), LXXVII (March, 1930), 360.

19. Ludwig Lewisohn, *Goethe—The Story of a Man* (New York, 1949), I, xii.

20. Barker Fairley, as cited, p. 272.

21. See George Santayana, *Egotism in German Philosophy* (New York, 1940), pp. v, vii.

22. George Santayana, *Three Philosophical Poets* (Cambridge, Mass., 1944), pp. 8, 139, 195, 142, 158.

23. Hermann J. Weigand, "Editor's Note," *CW,* p. 38.

24. S. Kirson Weinberg, *Culture and Personality—A Study of Four Approaches* (Washington, D. C., 1958), p. 45.

25. Clyde Kluckhohn, *Mirror for Man* (New York and Toronto, 1949), pp. 197, 226, 264.

26. Reported under UPI dateline, *Detroit Free Press* for February 16, 1960.

27. Louis H. Sullivan, *The Autobiography of an Idea* (New York, 1956), p. 198.

28. Lester G. Crocker, *An Age of Crisis* (Baltimore, 1959), pp. 181, 196-97.

29. See Edwin H. Zeydel, *Poems of Goethe* (Chapel Hill, 1957), pp. 82-83.

30. *Die Wahlverwandschaften,* I. Teil, 5. Kap., *JA,* 21:46.

31. *Wilhelm Meisters Wanderjahre,* 2. Buch, 11. Kap., *JA,* 20:47.

32. The same, 2. Buch, 7. Kap., *JA,* 19:279.

33. *Wilhelm Meisters Lehrjahre,* 8. Buch, 3. Kap., *JA,* 18:289.

34. *Dichtung und Wahrheit,* 2. Teil, 9. Buch, *JA,* 23:207.

35. The same, 3. Teil, 14. Buch, *JA,* 24:194.

36. "Winckelmann," in "Schriften zur Kunst," *JA,* 34:111. For the same idea, see Goethe's letter to Wilhelm von Humboldt, cited by Berthold Biermann, *Goethe's World* (New York, 1949), pp. 412 ff.

37. Goethe to Lavater, ca. September 20, 1780. See *Gedenkausgabe der Werke, Briefe und Gespräche Goethes,* ed. Ernst Beutler, 18 (Zürich, 1951): 532.

38. *Wilhelm Meisters Wanderjahre,* 5. Buch, 3. Kap., *JA,* 18:13.

39. See L. A. Willoughby, "Literary Relations in the Light of Goethe's Principle of 'Widerspiegelung,'" *Comparative Literature,* I (Fall, 1949), 309-23.

40. Frederic Wertham, *The Show of Violence* (New York, 1949).

41. Theodor Reik, *Listening with the Third Ear* (New York, 1949).

42. Editha and Richard Sterba, *Beethoven and His Nephew* (New York, 1954).

43. Johann Peter Eckermann, *Conversations with Goethe* (London, 1930), p. 392.

44. *Dichtung und Wahrheit,* 4. Teil, 20. Buch, *JA,* 25:1216.

45. For the history and interpretation of this amazing and difficult poem, see Martin Schütze, *Goethe's Poems* (Boston, 1916), pp. 195-98; and Julius Zeitler (ed.), *Goethe-Handbuch,* I (Stuttgart, 1916), 43-45.

46. Edwin H. Zeydel, *Poems of Goethe,* pp. 74-77.

47. See, for example, Ewald E. Boucke, *Goethes Weltanschauung auf historischer Grundlage* (Stuttgart, 1907); Karl Viëtor, *Goethe the Thinker* (Cambridge, Mass., 1950); Wolfgang Yourgrau, "Reflections on the Natural Philosophy of Goethe," *Philosophy,* XXVI (January, 1951), 69-84.

48. *Die Kampagne in Frankreich,* Pempelfort, November, 1792, *JA,* 28:155. Cited in *CW,* p. 129.

49. *Principes de philosophie zoologique,* 2. Teil (1832), *JA,* 39:233. Cited in *CW,* p. 1311.

50. *Über Farbentheorie,* Didaktischer Teil (1801), *JA,* 40:83. Cited in *CW,* p. 128.

51. *Die guten Weiber* (1801), *JA,* 16:309. Cited in *CW,* p. 128.

52. "Erläuterungen zu dem aphoristischen Aufsatz die Natur" (1828), *Gedenkausgabe der Werke, Briefe u. Gespräche Goethes,* ed. Ernst Beutler, 16 (Zürich, 1949) : 925-26. See also *JA,* 39:3-6, 349-50. Cited in *CW,* p. 130.

53. *Wilhelm Meisters Wanderjahre,* 2. Buch, 9. Kap. (1829), *JA,* 20:25. Cited in *CW,* p. 130.

54. Hempel edition, *Goethes Werke,* cited in Boucke, *Goethes Weltanschauung auf historischer Grundlage,* pp. 248-49. See also Eckermann, 6:54 for corroboration of Goethe's awareness of the poetic and symbolic character of his terms.

55. *Wilhelm Meisters Wanderjahre,* 2. Buch, 4. Kap., *JA,* 19:231.

56. *Wilhelm Meisters Lehrjahre,* 8. Buch, 6. Kap., *JA,* 18:328.

57. *Maximen und Reflexionen* (*Wanderjahre*), *JA,* 4:218.

58. Letter to Carl Ernst Schubarth, July 9, 1820, *WA,* IV:33:100.

59. Edwin H. Zeydel, *Goethe, The Lyrist* (Chapel Hill, 1955), p. 143.

60. "Nach Falkonet und über Falkonet," *WA,* I:37:321.

61. Letter to Sulpiz Boisserée, September 25, 1827, *WA,* IV:43:77. See also Goethe's letter of January 22, 1832, to Melchior Meyr, and the essay "Wohlgemeinte Erwiderung," *JA,* 38:240.

62. See Walter A. Kaufmann, "Goethe's Faith and Faust's Redemption," *Monatshefte für Deutschen Unterricht,* XLI (November, 1949), 365-75.

63. "Dem Herzog Bernard," *JA,* 2:237-38.

64. See note 15, above.

65. Translated by John F. Ebelke in Conrad P. Homburger and John F. Ebelke, *Foundation Course in German* (Boston, 1958), p. 258. For a translation by Stephen Spender, see Thomas Mann (ed.), *The Permanent Goethe* (New York, 1948), p. 655.

66. Barker Fairley, "Goethe—the Man and the Myth," in Arnold Bergstraesser (ed.), *Goethe and the Modern Age* (Chicago, 1950), p. 37.

V. The Growth of Self-Insight

1. *Experience and Nature* (New York, 1925), pp. 284-85.

2. *The Meaning of Meaning* (New York, 1923), p. 1174.

3. *Language: An Enquiry into Its Meaning and Function,* ed. Ruth N. Anshen (New York, 1949), p. 81.

4. William H. Kilpatrick, "We Learn What We Live," in *Freedom and Public Education,* ed. O. Melby and Morton Puner (New York, 1953), p. 42.

5. *Interpretation in Teaching* (New York, 1938), p. 18.

6. *Trends in Psychoanalysis* (London, 1951), p. 293.
7. Raynor C. Johnson, *The Imprisoned Splendour* (New York, 1953), p. 410.
8. J. L. Spalding, *Means and Ends of Education* (Chicago, 1909), p. 87.
9. Preface to *The Nature of Experience* (Oxford, 1959).
10. Anna Freud, *Indications for Child Analysis* (New York, 1945), I, 128.
11. C. K. Ogden and I. A. Richards, *The Meaning of Meaning* (New York, 1923), p. 262.
12. *Interpretation in Teaching* (New York, 1938), p. 230.
13. *The Art of Learning* (New York, 1931), p. 30.
14. *Interpretation in Teaching,* p. 6.
15. *Human Speech* (New York, 1930), p. 249.
16. Leonard Carmichael, *The Making of Modern Mind* (Houston, Texas, 1956), p. 88.
17. *Science and Sanity* (Lakeville, Conn., 1949), p. 41.
18. McGregor Health Foundation, Medical Director's Report to Trustees (1954), p. 15.
19. George Humphrey, *The Nature of Learning in its Relation to the Living System* (New York, 1933), p. 101.
20. *What is Education?* (Boston, 1915), p. 142.
21. *Science and the Modern World* (Cambridge, Mass., 1932), pp. 68-69.
22. Hans Reichenbach, *The Rise of Scientific Philosophy* (Berkeley, Cal., 1951), p. 326.
23. *Education for Freedom* (Baton Rouge, La., 1943), p. 22.
24. Julian M. Drachman, *Studies in the Literature of Natural Science* (New York, 1930), pp. 302-3.
25. *The Meaning of Psychology* (New York and London, 1926), p. 156.
26. William C. Bagley, *The Educative Process* (New York, 1916), p. 22.
27. *Science, Religion and Reality,* ed. Joseph Needham (New York, 1955), p. 255.
28. *The Logical Syntax of Language* (New York, 1937), p. xiii.
29. Borden P. Bowne, *Introduction to Psychological Theory* (New York, 1886), p. 3.
30. The same, p. 12.
31. J. H. van der Hoop, *Conscious Orientation* (New York, 1939), p. 96.
32. Daly King, *The Psychology of Consciousness* (New York, 1932), p. 245.
33. *A History of Medical Psychology* (New York, 1941), pp. 24-25.
34. *Physics: The Elements* (Cambridge, 1920), p. 264.

# *Biographical Notes*

HAROLD A. BASILIUS, Ph. D., is professor of German at Wayne State University and director of the Wayne State University Press. Born in Toledo, Ohio, in 1905, Dr. Basilius attended Concordia College, Fort Wayne, Indiana, and Concordia Theological Seminary, St. Louis, Missouri, receiving his B. D. degree from the seminary in 1928. His postgraduate work was done at Ohio State University where he received his M. A. degree in 1929 and Ph. D. degree in 1935. He taught German at Ohio State, Capital University, and the University of Chicago during the years 1929-36. From 1936-49 Dr. Basilius played a major role in the development of a humanities program at Wayne. He was professor and chairman of Wayne's German Department, 1936-41; chairman of its humanities program, 1941; chairman of its Foreign Language Committee, 1943-49; administrative head of the Departments of Ancient and Slavic Languages and Literature, 1943-49. He held the Leo M. Franklin Lectureship in Human Relations, 1953-54. His most recent book is *Contemporary Problems in Religion,* Wayne State University Press, 1956.

JOHN M. DORSEY, M. D., was professor and chairman of the Wayne State University Department of Psychiatry when he was chosen Leo M. Franklin Memorial Lecturer for 1959-60. He has just recently been honored with appointment to the post of University Professor

Born in Clinton, Iowa, in 1900, he was educated at the University of Iowa, receiving his M. D. degree in 1925. He was a member of the University of Michigan Department of Psychiatry from 1928-38; and, as Rockefeller Fellow, went to the University of Vienna and Vienna Psycholanalytic Institute, 1935-37, for postgraduate training. From 1946 to 1961 he was chairman of Wayne's Department of Psychiatry and head of psychiatry, Detroit Receiving Hospital. His other professional activities include being chief of psychiatry and neurology, Children's Hospital of Michigan; physician-in-chief, McGregor Center, a hospital for health education and rehabilitation; member of the teaching staff, Harper Hospital; chairman since 1951 of Detroit's Mayor's Committee for the Rehabilitation of Narcotics Addicts; member, Health Committee, Detroit Commission on Children and Youth; former director, Child Guidance Division, Children's Fund of Michigan. For fifteen years he was a member of the Highland Park Board of Education. Dr. Dorsey has written extensively in the fields of education, psychoanalysis, psychiatry, and neurophysiology; with Walter H. Seegers he is co-author of *Living Consciously: The Science of Self,* published by Wayne State University Press in 1959. Dr. Dorsey is a Life Fellow of the American Psychiatric Association.

BERNARD MAYO, Ph. D., has been professor of American history at the University of Virginia since 1940. Born in Lewiston, Maine, in 1902, he was educated at Johns Hopkins University, receiving his Ph. D. degree in 1931. He was a lecturer at American University in 1928-29; associate professor of American history and dean of the School of Economics at National University, 1929-33;

lecturer of American history, Graduate School, Georgetown University, 1937; visiting professor, Harvard University, 1946-47. Professor Mayo is a member of the American Historical Association, the Society of American History, and of the Southern Historical, Mississippi Valley Historical, Virginia Social Science, and Albemarle County Historical Associations. He is a member of the advisory committee for the publishing of the Thomas Jefferson papers by the Princeton University Press. The University of Virginia awarded him its annual Phi Beta Kappa prize in 1960. Professor Mayo is the author of several books, including *Myths and Men: Patrick Henry, George Washington, Thomas Jefferson,* 1959; *Jefferson Himself: The Personal Narrative of a Many-Sided American,* 1942; *Thomas Jefferson and His Unknown Brother, Randolph,* 1942; *Instructions to the British Ministers to the United States from 1791 to 1812,* 1941; and *Henry Clay, Spokesman of the New West,* 1937.

MILTON ROSENBAUM, M. D., is professor and chairman of the Department of Psychiatry, Albert Einstein College of Medicine, Yeshiva University; director of psychiatric services, Bronx Municipal Hospital Center; and visiting professor, acting director and organizer of the Department of Psychiatry, Hadassah Medical School, Hebrew University, Jerusalem. Born in 1910, in Cincinnati, Ohio, he was graduated in 1934 from the University of Cincinnati College of Medicine. From 1946-55 he was director of psychiatry at Jewish Hospital, Cincinnati; and he was a member of the Dean's Committee in Psychiatry, V. A., University of Cincinnati, 1948-55. Dr. Rosenbaum was consultant in psychiatry to the Surgeon-General, U. S.

Army, 1948-49-51; training analyst, Chicago Psychoanalytic Society, 1950-55; and supervising analyst, Chicago Institute for Psychoanalysis, 1950-55. In 1958-59 he was president of the American Psychosomatic Society, and he has been a member of the Training Committee, National Institute of Mental Health, since 1956. Dr. Rosenbaum is the author of more than eighty publications in the fields of psychiatry, psychoanalysis, psychosomatic medicine, and neurology.

WILBERT SNOW, L. L. D., LITT. D., "Poet of the Maine Coast," was born in 1884, on White Head Island, Maine. He was graduated from Bowdoin College in 1907 and went to Columbia University as Longfellow Fellow the following year. He received his M. A. degree from Columbia in 1910. As a young man he was a reindeer agent and teacher of Eskimo in Alaska and an artillery officer in World War I. For more than thirty years he taught English and debating at New York University, Bowdoin College, Williams College, the University of Utah, Reed College, Indiana University and Wesleyan University. He was lieutenant-governor, 1945-46, and governor, 1946-47, of Connecticut. Now retired professor of English at Wesleyan, he has recently been a State Department lecturer in twenty nations of Europe, Asia, and the Near East, explaining the American way of life and American culture. His books of poetry include *Maine Coast,* 1923; *The Inner Harbor,* 1926; *Down East Poems,* 1932; *Before the Wind,* 1938; *Maine Tides,* 1940; *Sonnets to Steve,* 1957; and *Spruce Head,* 1959.

The manuscript was edited by Barbara Woodward and the book was designed by Richard Berube. The type face for the text is Linotype Baskerville, cut in 1931 by the Mergenthaler Linotype Company and based on a face originally designed by John Baskerville between 1750 and 1758. The display face is Bulmer, which is a replica of a type face originally designed by William Martin for William Bulmer about 1790.

This book is printed on Warren's Olde Style Antique White Wove paper made by the S. D. Warren Company, and bound in Fromson Orban Company's Elephant Hide Paper over boards. Manufactured in the United States of America.